M000192074

Carol Duncombe was born in Northampton. She has two sisters, Hilary and Sue, and two brothers, Martin and Barry. Carol is married to Richard and has two daughters, Charlotte and Emma. Charlotte has a daughter, Evee, and Emma has twin boys named George and Edward. Carol worked as a midwife for 45 years and delivered over 2000 babies.

I dedicate this book to my husband, Richard, my daughters and their partners, Charlotte and Justin, Emma and my gorgeous grandchildren twins, George and Edward, and Evee. I would also like to include the wonderful staff and children at Olney Infant Academy.

Carol Duncombe

# MORE MEMOIRS OF A MIDWIFE

AUSTIN MACAULEY PUBLISHERS™

LONDON • CAMBRIDGE • NEW YORK • SHARJAH

Copyright © Carol Duncombe 2022

The right of Carol Duncombe to be identified as author of this work has been asserted by the author in accordance with section 77 and 78 of the Copyright, Designs and Patents Act 1988.

All rights reserved. No part of this publication may be reproduced, stored in a retrieval system, or transmitted in any form or by any means, electronic, mechanical, photocopying, recording, or otherwise, without the prior permission of the publishers.

Any person who commits any unauthorised act in relation to this publication may be liable to criminal prosecution and civil claims for damages.

All of the events in this memoir are true to the best of author's memory. The views expressed in this memoir are solely those of the author.

A CIP catalogue record for this title is available from the British Library.

ISBN 9781528991346 (Paperback)
ISBN 9781528991353 (ePub e-book)

www.austinmacauley.com

First Published 2022
Austin Macauley Publishers Ltd®
1 Canada Square
Canary Wharf
London
E14 5AA

With thanks to Richard, family and friends for their
encouragement in writing this book.

I was called out to a home birth in a village, in a little cottage. The stairs led up to the 2<sup>nd</sup> floor and then I had to climb a ladder to reach the patient, who had a bedroom in the attic. My first thought was *I hope all goes well as it would be extremely difficult to get this lady down the ladder to be transferred into hospital.*

The lady was doing well and some time later, I called the 2<sup>nd</sup> midwife. Her face was a picture when she arrived. She was a fairly large midwife, who only just made it up the ladder. It was so funny to watch her creeping around this tiny room. Our equipment was brought up the ladder by the husband and fortunately, the lady did very well and went on to deliver normally some hours later.

The fun began when we had to descend the ladder. The husband went first and we handed him the equipment, then I descended followed by my colleague, who was more worried about us looking up her skirt than getting down safely. I did not help as I was laughing. I just wish I could have recorded it.

# Remote Locations

For most of my career I worked in a rural area, covering villages and small hamlets. One of my ladies lived on a farm, which was approximately two miles up a fairly small track, with many bends and turns. I was lucky that when I visited I did not meet another vehicle coming towards me as it would have been very difficult to move to one side or reverse to let it past.

My colleague was not so lucky. She visited the farm on a rainy day and the road to the farm was fairly horrendous. She eventually arrived at the house, but had to be given a brandy as she was so distressed. I felt so sorry for her she was a fairly new midwife, who had just started on community and worked usually in a town area.

The farmer drove her car to the main road for her, but she was really traumatised by her experience and asked to be transferred back into the hospital as soon as possible as she thought she would have a nervous breakdown if she had to do any visits in such an area again.

She got her wish and returned back into the hospital environment to work. Every time I saw her after this, she told me that I deserved a medal for working where I did and she had no wish to return to my area. Oh dear. I assured her she had been unlucky with the weather and most of my ladies did not live in such a remote area. She was not convinced and told me she would never wish to work on community again. Poor girl was really traumatised by her experience.

Shortly after this experience, she was asked to work on community again as we were extremely short staffed. She agreed for a short time, but was unfortunately taken unwell in a patient's house and had to be rescued by a manager. The poor girl had a breakdown. Unfortunately, she did not return to midwifery and I do feel that if they had left her working in the hospital, she would still be working in the profession. What a waste of a good midwife.

# Breastfeeding

It was Easter Friday and I was visiting a lady, who had just had her third baby. I had met her during her pregnancy and she had told me that she really wanted to breastfeed. She had had a lot of difficulties with her first two children and was desperate to breastfeed this baby.

I told her I would do all I could to help her to do this. I arrived at the house to find a National Childbirth Trust breastfeeding member helping her. I sat quietly and listened with interest to information she was being given.

This went on for about half an hour and the baby was not fixing on the breast at all and the woman was becoming distressed.

I asked her if she would like me to help and she asked me to do this. I approached her and sat her comfortably on the sofa with a pillow on her lap. I then asked her if she minded me handling her breast. She told me she was fine with this. I took the baby, placed it on its side facing the mother and when the baby opened its mouth, gently pushed it onto the breast. Thankfully, the baby started to suckle and the woman was ecstatic.

The consultant said I was cruel and should let the baby find the nipple itself. I told her that this was very frustrating for the baby and the mother and sometimes you need to intervene to help out. This did not go down very well, especially when the husband called it the open and ram technique. My reply was the baby is feeding well, the mum is very happy, so I see no harm in this approach.

The lady was so happy her baby was feeding and told me if I had not arrived she would have given up as she and her baby were getting distressed.

This lady breastfed her baby successfully for nearly a year. Good for her.

# New Dads

I have met many interesting people throughout my career, but one I remember with a lot of doubt that he was ready to be a father. The lady was lovely and had an uneventful pregnancy and went on to deliver a beautiful baby boy.

My first visit to them was a little unsettling. The lady was doing very well looking after herself and her baby but her husband was struggling. He told me he had been shopping that morning for ear muffs, as the baby had kept him awake! I was a little shocked but told him babies cannot tell you what they need, so they cry. This was not an answer for him and he shortly after, left her and his baby and moved in with his previous wife. Words fail me.

The lady was obviously very shocked and sad, but coped really well on her own as she had a lot of support from her family. Somehow, I think she was better off without him. After a while, the lady moved back to her parent's home so that they could help her when she returned to work.

# Student Nurses

Student nurses as part of their training used to work with midwives for a short time during their training. This does not happen anymore but I had many students, who I enjoyed taking around with me.

One student stood out. He was young, cocky and not very professional. I worked with him during a hot spell one summer and he turned up to work in shorts, which I found a bit unprofessional. We had a lot of visits to do and during the first visit, he told the lady I was old enough to be his mother and I treated him like a child. I had a chat with him when we were in the car about being professional and not making comments about people's houses or décor. I was told his mother was a nursing manager and he knew how to behave.

I must admit I beg to differ. He asked for drinks, he sat himself down without being invited to sit and when I asked him if he would like to see a caesarean scar with the ladies consent, he told me no he was here to watch not to do anything. This was one student I was glad to see the back off and I do wonder if he progressed in his chosen career.

# The Need to Breathe Fresh Air

I was covering a clinic for a colleague, who was off sick and I think it is the only time in my career I have had to leave the room to get some fresh air.

A lady arrived bringing an aroma with her, she was from the local gypsy site and the state of her was awful. She was filthy and smelt really bad. I took her blood pressure and tested her urine and then asked her if I could examine her. Oh my goodness! Her abdomen was filthy and the smell was overwhelming. After a few minutes, I had to excuse myself to breathe some clean air. I did finish the appointment, but was not unhappy when she left. The next patient wrinkled her nose, when she came in the room and I spent the rest of the clinic apologising for the smell in the room. I had found this quite shocking as the gypsies I had previously come into contact with were extremely clean, when I had visited them and I had noticed how shining clean their caravans were. I thankfully never had to visit this lady in her caravan but, I imagine it would not have been a pleasant visit.

# I Cannot Be Pregnant

I met a lovely lady who was stunned that she was pregnant. She had been married for 15 years and had had all sorts of tests in a bid to get pregnant. When this didn't help, she and her husband adopted four children, all from different parts of the world. Then she got pregnant. This obviously was a great surprise for her and her husband, but they were thrilled and she had a lovely normal pregnancy and a beautiful baby girl. The way they made all the children feel part of their family was lovely to see and I often saw them all out and about together.

# More Births

The phone still rang in the middle of the night and off I would go to a home birth.

It was three am in the morning, when the phone had disturbed my sleep. I was called to help in the unit as they were very busy. I arrived on the labour ward to be asked to go into room (7), where the sound of screaming was coming from. I entered the room to face a lady who was on the bed screaming her head off, a father who looked terrified and a mother who was shouting at the girl to stop screaming.

My first instinct was to stop the noise. I approached the lady, introduced myself and told them I was there to help them. That went down a storm. We want a doctor who can do a section not any old midwife I was informed. I asked to look at the ladies notes and asked why she wanted a section? I was informed that the lady had no intention of giving birth through her fanny (her words) and that she wanted the baby out by the sun roof.

This was the ladies first baby and she was in early labour and finding it very difficult to cope. I offered her the gas and air and talked her through her next few contractions, so that she would relax and become a little more amenable to me being there. It became obvious that the girl's mother had terrified her about giving birth, telling her she would be cut from ear to ear, and shouted at to push and would never be the same again.

I reasoned with her and told her mum that she needed her support and that what had happened to her was not going to happen to her daughter. The atmosphere in the room was quite difficult and I asked her if she had been to any classes and did she know what happened during labour? She told me she had not been to any classes and had learnt about what happens from her mum.

Her mum had informed her that she would be screamed at to push, when the time came and would then be cut to get the baby out. I assured her that I had no intention of screaming at her or cutting her and that she could breathe the baby out slowly, so that she did not tear. I asked her to listen whilst she was quiet to what was going on in the unit. I can't hear anything she told me and I told her that other ladies were giving birth and no one was screaming or crying.

Slowly and surely, the lady started to trust me and she continued to use the gas and air to good effect, becoming more relaxed as time went on. Even her mother was keeping quiet and her husband was looking less afraid, that was until she needed to push. Then, all hell broke loose.

The poor girl was beside herself. She was so frightened. I had to start the reassuring game all over again. After what seemed like ages, she calmed down and began cooperating and did really well. She breathed her baby out and sustained no tear and thankfully, all was quiet apart from a crying baby. The lady was really pleased with the outcome and turned to her mother and told her that she had frightened her for nothing. I tried to explain that times have changed and that her mum was obviously traumatised by her birth, so perhaps her doing so well would make her mums worries fade into the background. Thankfully after this birth, I was able to go home to my lovely comfortable bed.

# The Cats Had Kittens

I visited a lady I had never met before. She had just delivered her first baby and was very excited. She had a beautiful baby. Also, her cat had had kittens so the house was very busy. All was well and I arranged to see her the following day.

When I visited the next day, the lady was sitting very uncomfortably. So, I asked her if I could look at her stitches to make sure they were healing well. I had a shock when I looked. The day before her suture line had been fine. Today, there were no stiches to see, they had come apart. I asked her what she had been doing to try to ascertain what had happened? She informed me she had had sex the night before and that must be what had done it. I was shocked to say the least. The poor girl had only given birth 3 days earlier, so this to me was unusual to say the least. I was informed that her husband had wanted sex so she obliged! I told her that it would have to heal on its own now and that could take a while. She asked me to talk to her husband, who apparently had shown disregard for how uncomfortable this had been for her.

The husband was unrepentant and told me that he needed his conjugal rights and he didn't see why he couldn't have them. I talked to him about the birth process and the need for her to be able to rest and recuperate from the birth. His reply was that he had needs too and it was no business of mine or anyone else what they did in their own home. I was fairly shocked by his attitude, but told him that if he continued to expect sex she would never heal and that was totally unfair to her.

I visited them a few days later and fortunately, the girl was healing well and being given time to do this. She also told me that her husband had been very good to her, since I spoke to him and was obviously feeling ashamed that he had acted as he had. Fortunately, he had not wanted her to have sex since I had last visited. Thank goodness for that. I had been thinking about her constantly for the last few days.

# Pre-Eclampsia

It was my evening 'ante natal class'. The ladies and their partners were arriving. We sat around chatting and talking about labour and I could see that one of the girls was looking really pale. I didn't want to draw attention to her as she was quite shy, so waited until the break, when I had made them all a cup of tea and asked her if she was feeling well. She told me she had a headache and felt a little under the weather. I took her into a room and took her blood pressure and asked her for a urine sample. Her blood pressure was high and she had a lot of protein in her urine, so I rang the hospital and asked them to see her. I told her that I would catch up with her in the morning and off she went with her husband.

I arrived at the hospital the next morning and went to the day assessment unit to find out what had happened to her. I was told she had been admitted to the labour ward with very high blood pressure, so I made my way there. It was fortunate for her that she had come to the class as she had been very unwell during the night and had been delivered. Her baby was well and her blood pressure was coming down nicely. Her husband had stayed with her overnight and asked me how I knew she was unwell. This is the beauty of looking after your own patients I told him, I knew what she normally looked like so it was easy for me to see that she had a problem. Fortunately, she recovered very quickly and was home one week later with her baby and although, it had been delivered at 36 weeks, it had no problems and did very well. It took nearly six weeks for her blood pressure to get back to normal.

# Difficult Decisions

Many years ago, I visited a lady for another midwife who was on a day off and was quite unsettled about the situation going on in the house. The father opened the door and invited me in. I chatted to the lady and asked her how she and her baby were. The husband stood over me the entire time and made me feel quite uncomfortable. The lady seemed well, but told me that her ten-day old baby was not feeding well. I asked if I could weigh the baby to see how he was doing. I was allowed to do this, but was not allowed to undress it. I was quite concerned to see that the baby had lost weight even when fully dressed, and seemed quite distressed.

I asked when the baby had last fed and was told 3 hours before, so I suggested that they should make up a feed and I would observe the baby with its bottle. The father grunted, but allowed his wife to go to the kitchen to do this. The baby seemed to feed quite well, but did seem very uncomfortable. I asked if I could examine the baby and was told in no uncertain terms no, he is fine and having his feed. I told them I was not happy to discharge them, but that they should feed the baby every 3 hours and I would make sure they had a visit the next day.

I was feeling quite unsettled about this visit, so went into the lady's doctors' surgery and spoke to her 'General Practitioner' (GP). He knew the family and said he would visit after he had finished his surgery.

I later had a phone call from that GP telling me that he had admitted the baby to the hospital and it had been found to have 3 broken bones. I was so upset and the GP was also very shocked. It turned out that the husband was very controlling and had been very rough when handling the baby. His poor wife was terrified of him. The lady had a good support system around her with her parents and sister and several weeks later, she was able to take her baby home with her. Her husband was not allowed to see or hold the baby and was prosecuted for his part in this poor baby's life.

It shows you that gut instinct can be right. I was so pleased and thankful that I had spoken to the GP, who was very supportive to the mother and I must say; to me. Thankfully, this is a rare event and most midwives don't have to deal with things like this very often.

# Milk Stout

On a lighter note, I visited a couple who had had their first baby. The lady was breastfeeding and telling me that the baby wasn't sleeping at all and she was finding it very difficult. I talked to her about her diet and in those days, I suggested that the mum drink milk stout to make her milk richer. I left them after we had discussed other things they could do to try to settle the baby, telling them I would visit the next day.

When the husband opened the door, his first words were that it didn't work and the baby wouldn't drink it. I was a bit confused by this and said wouldn't drink what? The stout he told me. He had put it in a bottle and tried to feed it to the baby. Oh my goodness! I was dumbfounded that parents would do that, but they thought that is what I meant. If I ever said that to a lady after that, I made sure she knew it was for her and not her baby.

# Baby Monitors

I visited a lady who had just had her first baby and her mother-in-law had come to help. I could tell when I went into the house that the lady was quite tense and near to tears, so I suggested that we went upstairs to have a chat.

We went into the lady's bedroom and she proceeded to tell me that she was struggling as her mother-in-law did not agree with anything that she was doing with the baby and was literally driving her mad. I talked to her about the need to ensure that she was in control and the way she was looking after her baby was great. Her baby was breastfeeding well and putting on weight. We discussed what she could do to assert herself and talked about her speaking to her husband, so that she had some back up with her mother-in-law.

All of a sudden, I realised that the baby monitor which was in the room was relaying to her mother-in-law exactly what we had been saying. I quietly pointed to the monitor and the mum was horrified. I then went on to say that her mother-in-law was only trying to help and that she should talk to her about what she wanted her to do to help her. The girl fortunately caught on to the problem and went on to say that she was very fond of her mother-in-law and was very grateful for all the help she was giving to her and her husband and felt awful that she was not coping.

I told her she was like any new mum who needed help, but had to make her own decisions about the way she looked after her baby. I gave the girl a hug and told her she was doing really well and eventually we went downstairs, obviously not saying anything about what we knew the lady had heard. I told the lady I would visit her the next day and I left.

I visited the next day and was met by a lady, who was looking much happier. We went upstairs and made sure the monitor was switched off and she told me that her mother-in-law had been really supportive since the incident and had let her get on with the care of the baby and restricted her help to cooking cleaning and supporting.

Phew! That was a relief. It could have been a very different outcome. This had been a lesson for me too. I always after that, informed the ladies about the perils of baby monitors and to make sure that if they wanted to rant to anyone they should make sure that they were turned off and not broadcasting their tirade.

I had another much funnier run in with a baby monitor. I was visiting a lady, who had told me during her pregnancy that her mother-in-law had volunteered to come to her house after she had delivered. This lady was very fond of her mother-in-law, but told me she was very posh and talked as if her mouth was full of marbles.

After this lady delivered, I attended the house and was invited in by the said lady. The girl was doing extremely well with looking after her baby and was obviously besotted with her baby girl.

The mother-in-law excused herself and said she was going to the baby's nursery to dust it and put away some washing.

Soon after this I heard a funny noise, I looked at the mum and she was also wondering what the noise was. Then it happened again much louder and longer. We both realised at the same moment that it was the mother-in-law farting. We were both laughing and trying to stop, when the ladies husband walked in. Obviously, he wanted to know what was funny. At that point it happened again.

Fortunately, the husband thought it was funny too and said his mother had always had a problem with wind, but had always denied she had a problem.

At that point, the mother-in-law emerged back into the room and I was wondering if anything would be said. I hoped not as I thought she would be embarrassed.

Nothing was said and I finished the visit and winked at the mum and told her I would see the next day to weigh the baby. I must admit it made me chuckle all day.

# Difficult Times

My youngest sister Sue had a difficult delivery. She was having her first baby and the pregnancy had gone well, but it was fairly obvious that her baby was going to be large. She went into labour and it was becoming obvious that she was running into difficulties, so she was offered an epidural. She was happy to have this and the deed was done. The anaesthetist sited the epidural and then left the room, fortunately leaving a midwife in the room with Sue.

It quickly became obvious Sue was unable to breathe for herself and obvious to the midwife that she needed help. This help came quickly and Sue was rapidly given a general anaesthetic for an emergency section.

One of the risks of an epidural is that it can be sited too high and can go up instead of down and this is a total emergency as the patient is unable to breathe for themselves. I have heard of this but have never seen it happen in any hospital that I have worked in. It is extremely frightening for the lady and her husband and can leave a lasting fear with the mother, which is very understandable.

Sue recovered well and had a beautiful son Mathew. Some months after the birth, it was obvious to me that she was finding it difficult to put what had happened to her behind her.

I suggested that she made an appointment with the anaesthetic department at the hospital to talk it through and I told her I would go with her for support.

An appointment was made and we attended the hospital for the appointment. The anaesthetist was extremely rude and told us we were wasting his time, he wanted to know what the problem was and I told him how traumatised Sue had been at the time. His answer was well you're alive, what are you wanting me to tell you?

I told him Sue needed reassurance that if she was ever to have another baby was it likely to happen again? His answer was probably not. I then ended the meeting and took her home.

The rules for epidural are clear and I have never seen them broken. An anaesthetist inserts the epidural, and then gives a test dose to make sure it is working as it should. They stay with the lady in the room until they are happy that the epidural is in the right place and is working as it should. I learnt after this meeting that the anaesthetist we had met with was always rude and was not liked at the hospital where he worked. I am sure he was good at his job, but patient safety and wellbeing should be at the top of his list. Not his ego.

If anyone is unhappy or left with any questions about their birth these days, it is good practice to have a follow up service in place to meet with the ladies and go through their questions, this always happened at the hospital where I worked and it is a good service.

# Birth Attendees

I met an American couple who were having their first baby. They had been quite surprised at the 'ante natal class', when I had told them that it was unusual to have more than two birth partners with them at the birth. Usually the husband and one other if wanted. They were quite concerned about this as they had wanted their whole family with them.

I have watched programmes from America, where in the delivery ward they sometimes have what seems a cheer leading crew with them. I told the couple that it was not a spectator sport, but if they wanted more family with them at the birth, they would have to discuss this with the Delivery Suite Coordinator. I told them they needed to discuss this between them and do what was right for them.

I spoke to this couple at their next 'ante natal appointment' and they told me that they had decided to be on their own for the delivery, but had arranged with the hospital that their family could wait at the hospital and come in to see the baby soon after the baby was born. As long as they were happy, I could see no problem with this.

I heard from the labour ward after she had delivered that they had 18 of this lady's relatives wanting to come in as soon as the baby was born. Wow! I thought when they said relatives, they meant their parents, not the world and his wife.

# Single Mum Delivery

Another night on call and another phone call. I was called to a home birth, where I found the mother in good labour and no partner, but three children who were in bed. I discussed with the mother what plans she had for her labour and who was going to look after her and her other children once the baby was born? The estate this family lived on was notorious for crime so I was a bit reluctant to leave the car, but as I couldn't take it into the house there was no option.

She seemed surprised that I was asking her that, she thought that she could manage on her own. I told her that once she had delivered, I could not leave her and her baby without any support. She informed me that this was why she had wanted a home birth as she had no support. Oh dear.

I told the lady let's just get this baby delivered and then we could sort something out for her. She was progressing very well and it came time to call for the second midwife. I rang the delivery suite and was told that the 2nd midwife was unable to be contacted. Lovely, just what you want to hear. I informed the coordinator of the situation and told her there was no way this lady would come into hospital as she had no one to look after her other children, so could they please send a hospital midwife out to support me?

I was told after a short time that a midwife would be joining me, so I prepared the lady for her delivery. Soon after this time, she wanted to push and the 2<sup>nd</sup> midwife had still not arrived. I went on to deliver the baby when the 2<sup>nd</sup> midwife phoned to say she was still at the hospital. I told her not to bother to come as the baby was born. It had been an hour and a half since I had rung the hospital, so I don't know why she did not leave earlier? Thankfully, all was well and I was ready to tuck the lady up with her baby to get some rest.

Fortunately, we had rung the lady's sister and she had agreed to come and help look after her. This should have been sorted out earlier, when her midwife had been to see her at 36 weeks to discuss her birth but fortunately, things had turned out well. When I spoke to this lady's midwife, she had been informed that the lady would have a relative in the house for the delivery, so was a bit cross that this had not happened. As I said to her, it all turned out well in the end so not to worry.

As a footnote from this delivery, my car still had four wheels when I left the lady.

# Funny Pictures

I remember visiting a couple who had just had their first baby. I had not met them before and they were so excited that their baby had arrived. The husband opened the door to me and invited me to sit in the lounge as his wife was just getting out of the shower.

Whilst I was sitting there, I was looking above the fireplace where a picture was hanging. It was something I hadn't seen before and was just about to get up and have a closer look, when the couple came into the room. Oh said the husband, I see your looking at our picture. Yes, I said. Well, he told me it was the baby's first poo. I was a bit gob smacked at the time, but must admit I had to laugh when I got back into my car. I had asked him how had he preserved the poo and he looked a bit shocked and said do you think I should have done that? I replied I really don't know it's something I have not come across before. His reply was well we like to be different. Each to their own, not something I would hang on my wall.

Edward and George

Rhys Jake and Chip

Evee

Eloise

Aaron Izaac Toby Bertie Arabella Arian All delivered at home by myself

Millie Ellie and Evie

Grace and George

Bertie Aaron arabella arcana izaak and Toby

# Weighing Scales

When I first started on community, we had scales that were like fishermen use to weigh their catch. We went on to have scales like kitchen, ones the base was separate from the top. I visited a lady who needed her baby to be weighed, when I realised I had not taken the top of the scales into the house. I went out to my car and suddenly realised I had left them at home. I had taken them home as the top seemed a bit scuffed, so I had cleaned them and obviously left them there.

I returned to the house to confess and we decided that we could adapt and use their cooking tray to weigh the baby. It worked but the mother told me at a later date that she had dreamt that she had put her baby in the oven on the baking tray. Oh dear, probably not the best idea I had come up with. The husband told me he had bought another baking tray so that they could save the one the baby had used to show him at a later date what they had done. I am sure he would have appreciated that on his 18$^{th}$ birthday.

# Peaceful Birth

Another night and another call. A home birth was ongoing about nine miles away from where I lived. I arrived at the house to be faced with a husband, who looked totally panic struck. I entered the house and said to the husband I hope you have put the kettle on. He asked me how much water I needed? I told him just enough to make a cup of tea.

This was their 2$^{nd}$ baby and they had delivered their first baby in a London Hospital and had not been happy with the delivery. The labour had been long and had ended with the baby being born in theatre, with help from doctors with forceps.

I asked them about what they wanted for this birth and was informed they wanted a nice quiet normal birth with no pain relief. Well that's what we will aim for I told them. I made the usual checks and found out that she was already 6 cm dilated, so was doing very well. I encouraged her to move around and do what she wanted to do and I would listen into baby regularly and we would wait to see what happened.

The husband was still quite anxious, so I talked to him and told him that I had no worries about the birth, the mum and baby were doing well and all was ready for the delivery, so just to relax and enjoy the moment. I asked him if they had got any thoughts about cutting the cord or whether they wanted to do skin to skin straight away or whether they wanted the baby to be dried off first?

This was discussed and suddenly the lady decided she felt pressure, so I called the 2$^{nd}$ midwife and just told the lady to do what her body was telling her to do. The lady asked me how she would know when to push. I told her people in comas have given birth, your body will know exactly where and when to push.

The second midwife arrived and was a bit of a chatter box. I spoke quietly to her and told her that the lady wanted to be quiet and we should keep the noise down. Bless her, she found it hard to keep quiet so I asked her if she had any gob stoppers. Fortunately, she took the hint and all was quiet.

Soon after this, the lady started to feel she wanted to push. I told her to do what she felt her body wanted her to do. So, she wanted to find a place where she felt comfortable to deliver. This was fine with me but I do wonder why women seem to find the smallest place possible to give birth. This happened to be half way up the stairs.

The 2$^{nd}$ midwife whispered to me she can't deliver here, too late it was happening, and quickly. I told the husband to sit on the stair with his wife so he could help steady her so she would not fall. He quickly did this and I stood below waiting for the baby to appear. A few pushes later, I could see the head, so told her to breathe and let the baby come on its own. Fortunately, this happened quickly as we were all in a bit of a precarious position. The head delivered slowly and with the next contraction the baby was born, and cried immediately.

We were sitting on the stairs; mum was cuddling baby and then we had to decide whether to stay where we were or to move to deliver the placenta? The lady decided she wanted to stay where she was so we awaited the appearance of the afterbirth. Fortunately, about ten minutes later, it appeared and we could all move to a safer place.

We went downstairs and the lady sat on the sofa with her baby and we made them a cup of tea. I took the tea into them only to find her and her husband both sobbing and unable to speak. I was worried that something was wrong, but when I could get any sense out of them, they told me they were so happy with the delivery that they couldn't stop crying. Bless them. They told me they would encourage all their friends to have home births. Let's hope they don't all deliver at the same time.

# Birth Plans

During one of my 'ante natal classes', I had a couple who were having their first baby. They were obviously very much in love and couldn't take their hands off one another. When we were talking about birth plans, I discussed with the class what they were? what they could write on them? and ways to accomplish this. I also told them that as they hadn't had babies before they should not be too specific, but to be amenable to their choices being changed.

Well, that went down with most of the class but for this loving couple, they insisted that they wanted a delivery with no pain relief, no doctors and the husband wanted to deliver the baby. I explained that this would be difficult to achieve, the pain relief part was fine. Having just midwives was great as long as everything was normal, but the husband would not be allowed to deliver the baby. He could help but it was against all the safety rules for him to actually deliver the baby. I also told them that they could have a water birth, during which he could get in the pool with her and help bring the baby to the surface once it was delivered. I suggested they go home and discuss what they wanted and I would discuss it at their next appointment.

The outcome to this birth was that they decided to have a water birth in the hospital. I was on call the night they delivered and was asked to go in and assist as labour ward was really busy. I arrived to find the lady in the pool contracting well. The husband at this point was out of the pool and encouraging her from the side of the pool.

The time came when she needed to push and that's when the problem started. I found out later that she had not had her bowels open for six days. Oh dear, well the floodgates opened when she started pushing. The sieve came in very useful for clearing the pool, but it became obvious that this was not going to be enough. The pool was becoming unhygienic for the woman and definitely not suitable to deliver in.

I said to the husband that we needed to get her out to deliver and he agreed with me. The lady was not happy with this, but when I told her that we could not expect her baby to delivery in dirty water, eventually she agreed with me.

We managed to get her out and she decided to deliver on the bed on all fours. Fortunately, soon after this the baby put in an appearance and all was well. Then I had to clear the pool. What a joy that was. It was disgusting and smelly and not the best job in the world but unfortunately, it had to be done. I was so happy when it was done and I could leave to go home. I found out later that the husband was grateful that I had done the clearing up and not asked him to help. The joys of being a midwife.

# Different Partners

I looked after a lady in a village who was having her $2^{nd}$ baby. I had visited her at home during her pregnancy and her partner had been with her. When she had delivered, I saw her and thought her partner looked different. I knew I had seen this man before, but I was sure it was not with the lady I was visiting. I was speaking to the health visitor shortly after this, about who had delivered and was due a visit from them and bought up this couple.

It was known in the village that this lady and her next-door neighbour had swapped partners recently, they had both had babies within a short time, but who was the father of each baby? No one seemed to know. As I said to the health visitor that as long as the mums and babies are happy and well, they can swap around as much as they like. People do sometimes live problematic lives and we do get to see some funny situations.

# Another Night On-Call, Another Home Birth with Dogs

I was sent to a lady who lived quite near where I lived. I arrived at the house, to find a lady upstairs on a double bed with 2 large noisy dogs with her on the bed. She informed me that she wanted the dogs to be with her as she delivered. This was fine. The problems began when I tried to examine the lady and the dogs did not like it. They growled and bared their teeth, which made me a bit wary. She told me that she wasn't moving and I would have to cope with it the best way I could. Great, just what I wanted to hear.

I tried to listen in to the baby on a regular basis, but it was really difficult. The dogs were growling and menacing and really quite frightening. The husband just said get on with it, that's what you're paid for.

After a few hours of this, it became evident that she was probably going to deliver shortly, so I called for the second midwife. I went downstairs to greet the midwife and to update her on what was happening. We went upstairs together and the situation was the same: two dogs, one woman and her husband. We coped as best as we could. It became obvious that this baby was not going to put in an appearance, without some outside help as the baby had turned into a posterior position. This means that the babies back had turned to be in line with the women's spine. This makes the delivery more difficult.

We discussed this with them and they agreed to be transferred into hospital.

An ambulance was called and came within a short time. Then the fun began. The woman was being protected by her dogs and none of us could get near her. We explained that there was no way she could take the dogs with her and that she obviously needed help. Eventually, the husband was able to remove the dogs from the situation and we scuttled as quickly as we could out to the ambulance.

The lady was admitted to the delivery suite and gave birth some hours later with the help of forceps. I was so pleased she was not one of my ladies and I would not have to visit them at home again. I did warn her midwives about the dogs and she phoned the woman and told her that the dogs needed to be in a different room, when she visited as she was allergic to them. I wish I had thought of that one.

I have no problem with most family dogs and don't expect people to put them away when I visit.

I was showing a new community midwife around my area and we went to visit a lady of mine who had a Labrador. The dog was typical puppy, a bit scatty but no problem. I was just telling the new midwife this when the door opened. I turned round to introduce the other midwife to my lady, when I realised she had disappeared.

I went into the house and did the visit and afterwards went back to my car. The other midwife was standing by the car and informed me that she did not like dogs. I told her that families with dogs had babies and she would have to get used to them or not work on community. I was told by her that she was scared of dogs and had been since she was a child. This is unfortunate, but unless you phone every patient before you visit them this could be a problem.

# Smoking During Delivery

I was called out to a home birth one night, so I called my student and arranged to pick her up on the way. When we arrived at the house, we were greeted by the lady and her husband who were hoping to deliver in their small lounge. This was fine, the problem was she was already asking for gas and air and they had an open fire. I explained that she could not have gas and air as this would be dangerous with an open fire. This was obviously disappointing for them, but I explained that once we had assessed her progress then she could have an injection for pain relief.

This was fine by the lady and during the examination it came out that she wanted a home birth because both she and her husband smoked and wished to do so during her labour. My student's mouth was wide open at this point. She could not believe it.

Fortunately, the examination found that she was progressing well, and it was too late for the injection. I called the second midwife and proceeded to get ready for the delivery. At this point, the husband asked my student if she wanted a fag. I wish I could have taken a picture of her face. She could not believe it and politely declined.

A few minutes later, the lady needed to push and I must admit I have never delivered anyone who was smoking during the delivery. I explained to them both that a smoky atmosphere was not good for the baby and they should try not to smoke around it. Their reply, it's our house, our baby. We will do what we like. There is no answer to that, but once the baby had arrived and they were having a cuddle, I discussed the risks of smoking with a baby. The risk is higher of cot death and chest complaints and failure to thrive. This fell on deaf ears.

We cleared up and left them to it some hours later. The discussion with the student on the way home was interesting. I had to explain to her that we are there to give the parents information and advice, but not to condemn them for the way they live. We would obviously encourage them to make healthier choices but it's up to them if they take that advice. All I wanted to do was go home and get my uniform into the wash as I felt I stank of cigarettes.

I was on my rounds some days later, when I was called to see the lady who had delivered at home a few nights earlier (The smoker). I was not far from the house so quickly made my way there.

When I walked into the house, I was faced with a very small room filled with relatives and so much cigarette smoke you could hardly see across the room. I was told the baby was not feeding well and seemed unwell. The baby was pale and limp and obviously unwell. I immediately called the GP, who I knew was just around the corner as I had seen him at another patient's house and told the husband to clear the room of relatives and open the windows. I took the baby and it was obviously very unwell. Fortunately, the GP arrived quickly and we thought we should get the baby to the hospital as soon as possible. The GP drove and I held the baby having to give it CPR on the way. We went straight into the casualty department and fortunately, the baby was successfully resuscitated and soon after, transferred to 'Oxford' with a complex heart condition.

The woman and her husband arrived at the hospital and the mum went in the ambulance with the baby.

A few days later, I was informed that the baby needed surgery and that the mother or father needed to go to the hospital to sign the consent form, but they couldn't get hold of them. I made my way to their house and they were in, so I informed them of what was happening and was told, we don't have the money to get there. I rang the hospital to see if I could get any help with this and was put through to the finance department, who arranged to fund the hospital visit. I then had to take them to the local hospital to get the money to go to 'Oxford'. I was actually a bit unsettled by all of this and felt that if they could afford to buy cigarettes they should be able to visit their baby. Unfortunately, it is up to the parents how they spend their money.

The outcome of this case was that the baby did well and was eventually able to go home to its parents. Whether they are still smoking I don't know, but I do know they would have been given strict instructions on how to treat their baby. I can only hope they listened.

# New Midwife

We had a new midwife starting on community and I was assigned to take her out with me as she would be working in a surgery fairly local to mine, so needed to learn the area.

It was a cold snowy day and we set off in good spirits. We did some local visits and then set off for a visit in a former stately home, which had been split into beautiful flats. The drive was long and slippery and I was driving slowly, but could see a four by four driving towards me at a much faster rate. I moved as far to the left as I could and my wheels skidded into a shallow ditch. We got out of the car and tried to push the car back onto the path, but that was not happening. The other midwife was wearing pink padded boots, which were ideal for the weather. I was wearing sturdy shoes not good at gripping the icy road. We were in hysterics, it was so comical but we realised we needed help, so we walked up the drive, found the patient and explained our predicament. Fortunately, the husband was amenable to helping us and came with his four by four and towed us out. We did manage to do the visit before he did this.

I worked with that midwife for many years and we often laughed about her initiation to community, she told me I had tried to kill her on her first day.

# The Parrot Delivery

I once did a home birth in a house where they had a parrot. I had heard about this parrot but had not met it.

The lady was doing well when I arrived and I was welcomed into the house and made a nice cup of tea to wake me up. She had decided to deliver in the lounge and that's when I met the parrot. I have never laughed so much during a delivery. The parrot's language was awful. It kept saying bugger me, over and over again. It coincided with each contraction it seemed and the lady and her husband were also laughing.

This lady did very well. Her contractions were coming regularly and every time one came, she walked around the room much to the delight of the parrot. Its eyes followed her around and frequently came out with "here we go again", it was absolutely hysterical to watch. I asked at one point if he could be quiet as my sides were aching with all the laughing but thankfully, he didn't stop and continued to comment throughout her labour.

The labour progressed well and it came time to ring for the 2$^{nd}$ midwife. Shortly after this, she arrived and was greeted with a wolf whistle and a cor. She looked quite shocked, but I told her not to fret it was just the parrot.

I was getting ready for the delivery and I could see the parrot was interested in what was going on, it was following me with its eyes with its head on one side with intermittent comments like cor or a wolf whistle. All of a sudden, the parrot commented that's the way to do it. Hilarious.

Soon after this the lady started to push and we got ready to deliver. The baby arrived to a bloody hell, well bugger me. We were all laughing so much we could not control ourselves. The lady sat on the sofa with her husband and new baby and thanked us for our help. I had to tell them I had not had such a laugh for a long time and hoped I would get to deliver her next baby. I must admit I laughed all the way home.

# Flu Clinic at the Surgery

It was clinic afternoon; it was also flu clinic. The surgery was very busy with older people coming in for their yearly flu injection.

I was running my clinic and half way through ran of some paperwork that I needed. I went to the cupboard to get it. I had to get through a line of pensioners. I had just reached where I needed to be, when I was chastised by an elderly lady for jumping the queue. I tried to reassure her that I was not intending to get in the way but needed to get to the cupboard. Bless her. No way, she told me I'm next, out of my way. Fortunately, at this time one of the GPs saw what was going on and came and saved me from the lady's wrath and her handbag, which she was waving in the air. I went back to my lady who was amused when I told her what had happened.

# Mastitis in Baby

I was doing my round of 'postnatal visits' and I visited a lady, who had given birth five days earlier to a baby boy. I was examining the baby, when the mum told me he seemed unsettled and fretful. He was looking well and was feeding well but did seem uncomfortable. I stripped his clothes off to examine him and looking at his chest was surprised to see that his breasts were very red and swollen and looked extremely painful. I took his temperature which was slightly raised. I told the mum I was going to inform the GP as I thought the baby had mastitis (infection of the breast tissue). I had never seen it before in a baby and when I rang the GP, he said that he thought that there was no chance it was mastitis but agreed to see it.

The outcome was the baby did have mastitis and was treated with antibiotics. This cleared up within a two-day period. The GP was shocked as he had never seen or heard of it before. Thankfully, this baby went on to do very well and the problem never recurred.

# Snakes in the House

I was on my way home after my clinic when I was asked to go to a home birth a few miles away. I told them I was not on call but apparently, I was the only one who had answered their phone. So, I agreed to go as long as I could be relieved as soon as possible as I had to attend a parent teacher evening. This was agreed so off I went.

I arrived at the house and the door was opened by a gentleman, who ushered me into the house. I was just about to follow him into the house, when I saw a very large snake wriggling up the corridor towards me. I quickly returned to the doorstep and told the man he would have to cage the snake if he wanted me to come in.

He wasn't very happy but agreed to do this. I was shocked that as he was scooping up the snake, a young child appeared and seemed underwhelmed with the snake. I did feel bad but there was no way I was going to share this birth with a snake.

When I eventually went into the house, the husband told me the snake was friendly and wouldn't hurt anyone. He went on to tell me it could swallow a child if it wanted to. It had the run of the house usually and was a pet to all the family. Each to his own.

Fortunately for my sanity, another midwife arrived after an hour and I was able to leave. The midwife was feeling the same way as I did about the snake being there, so I did not feel too bad that I had asked them to remove it. I must admit I was very happy when I was able to leave.

# Ice on the Road

I was called to a home birth in my local area. The roads were icy and it took me a while to get to her house. The lady was having her second baby and was doing very well when I arrived. One of the GPs I worked with, knew this lady well and had expressed a wish to be at the delivery. It was a really cold icy night and the weather was getting worse.

As the night progressed, the lady suddenly announced she felt she needed to push. I immediately rang the GP and was very surprised when he arrived some minutes later. I asked him how he had got there so quickly and he informed me he had driven from his home with his head out of the window as the windscreen was so icy. Bless him.

The lady obliged and delivered her baby shortly after this. We delivered the placenta and then settled down for a cup of tea whilst writing the notes. The GP was then able to leave and go home. I unfortunately, had to drive to the hospital to finish the paperwork and refill the bag. It was some hours later that I was able to go home to my bed.

# Sugar in Urine

It was time for my clinic. I had a full list and all was calm. Half way through the clinic, I had a lady who had a lot of sugar in her urine. I had the conversation about diet, but we couldn't pin point what was causing the problem. I made an appointment for her to have a fasting blood sugar. This has to be done after a 12 hour fast so obviously, I couldn't do it straight away.

I continued with my clinic and then received a phone call from the said lady. She told me she had been thinking about her diet and did I think it could be the two bottles of lemonade she drank every day.? I think we may have got to the bottom of the problem. I advised her to stop drinking it and to see me the following week. She did this and surprise, no sugar in her urine.

# Difficult Husband

I was asked in my capacity as a Supervisor, to visit a lady from another practise. She was having problems in her pregnancy. I was told she was having kidney problems and had a husband who was quite difficult.

Apprehensive, I knocked on the door and was eventually invited in. The husband was in attendance and questioned everything I asked the lady. He was quite aggressive and made me feel quite uncomfortable. The lady had needed to have a catheter inserted for the rest of her pregnancy to drain her urine, as she was having kidney problems. The husband thought it was a fuss about nothing and wanted it out as it got in the way when he wanted sex. I explained to them both how important it was for this to stay in place, but when I left I didn't think I had made any inroads into the problem.

I had just arrived at the hospital the next weekend, when I was told that the lady was in labour and they were having problems with the husband. I was asked to go to labour ward and try and reason with him. Just what I needed first thing in the morning.

I went into their room and asked how things were going. I knew that the baby was in distress and the lady was being advised to have a caesarean section. The lady was amenable for this to happen, but the husband was kicking up a fuss. I tried to reason with him, telling him that it was necessary for the baby to be delivered within a short time as it wasn't coping with the labour.

After a short time, he said he wasn't happy but he would accompany his wife to theatre for the birth of his baby. Phew! That was a relief.

Then the fun started. We took the lady to theatre and were getting her settled and pain free, when the husband forced his way into the room and started swearing and attacking the staff. It was total mayhem. The lady was crying and the next thing was that the police entered the room and arrested him.

This is the first and last time I ever saw anything like this happen. The man was banned from the maternity unit so did not get to meet his baby, until they both returned home three days later.

I was asked to do the postnatal visits unfortunately, and was not looking forward to it. A plan was made that I would ring a colleague when I was visiting and she would ring me shortly after this to see if I was safe.

It was fortunate that the husband made himself scarce during the visits so thankfully, all was well. I did see the man walking about the town in later weeks and wondered how their marriage could last after the mayhem he had caused. The lady and the baby did very well thankfully and although nothing was said to me about what had happened in the hospital, I did wonder what she thought about it. I would have kicked him into touch.

# Phantom Pregnancy

I was asked to do a clinic for a midwife who was on annual leave. The first lady to arrive was a booking. This is the first time we meet the lady and fill in her notes and decide the best plan of care for her. I introduced myself and congratulated her on her pregnancy. She told me she had come to get her pregnancy notes, so that she could go to the council to get a house. I informed the lady that she would be given her notes at the end of the appointment. I was informed that she had an appointment with the housing department in an hour, so I suggested that we get on with the notes so that she could make it to her appointment.

I was told in no uncertain terms that all she wanted was her notes and didn't want me to fill them in just give them to her. I informed her that I couldn't do this as blank notes would be no use to her.

Her answer to this was well, get a move on then. I started to go through the notes but was quite surprised when I asked her when the first day of her last period was? she told me she didn't have periods as she had an implant in her arm. I asked her if she had a positive pregnancy test and she told me she had so. I informed her that we should get an early scan to ascertain how far pregnant she was. She told me she didn't

69

want a scan, she just wanted her notes. I tried to tell her that having pregnancy notes did not mean she would be given a house.

I was feeling a little unsettled about all this as I had never heard of anyone falling pregnant with an implant in, so I excused myself and went to speak to the doctor who was on duty at the time. He told me that the girl wasn't pregnant and that she had been making appointments to see the midwife several times and she was just after a house.

Fortunately for me, the GP agreed to come into the room to talk to the lady. I was surprised when I returned to the room, the lady had disappeared and had thankfully left her notes behind.

I found out later that the lady had had several appointments with different midwives throughout the city and had succeeded in getting notes but had been found out when she went for a scan. I made it known in our community office what had happened so that she would not waste another midwife's time.

# Different Positions

I was visiting a lady who was quite concerned about her breastfeeding. She was convinced she did not have enough milk.

We had a chat about how the baby was feeding, how often and for how long? I offered to weigh the baby to see what progress he was making and she agreed with this.

The baby had put on a little weight but was still not back to his birth weight. I suggested that I should stay whilst she fed the baby and make sure that all was well.

The baby was due for a feed so this worked well. I told the lady to feed as she normally did and if I had any suggestions that would promote better feeding, I would talk to her about them.

The lady laid herself on her bed and positioned her baby over her shoulder with his head on her breast. I thought this was a weird way to position the baby but waited for a few minutes to see what happened before I made any comments.

It became clear that the baby was not feeding well, so I suggested that we repositioned the baby to see if that would help. The lady was quite reluctant to do this as she was comfortable. I pointed out that the baby was almost upside down trying to feed. This was not a good way for the baby to digest its milk.

I suggested that she could stay on her bed, then arrange her pillows so she was comfortable, then position the baby.

She agreed to this, but was still concerned she didn't have enough milk. I asked her if she minded me touching her breast and she said this was fine. I told her I would show her she had a good milk supply by expressing her breast.

I showed her how she could express her milk and she was really surprised when the milk shot across the room in a shower. Her face was priceless.

I then showed her how to position her baby in a better position. Once the baby was feeding, I asked the lady if she stood on her head to eat her meals. She laughed and said of course not, why would I?

I smiled and said well the baby was almost upside down in the former position, so would find it difficult to digest its milk.

The baby fed really well and we had a good laugh about her first position. She agreed that this feed felt a lot better than the others and she was very comfortable.

I left her to it and made arrangements to visit her three days later.

I called in to see this lady and the baby was feeding beautifully and had put on a lot of weight. The lady and her husband were really happy with their progress and told me that she would have stopped breastfeeding if I had not visited. Another happy patient.

# Antenatal Classes

I ran 'ante natal classes' and during the first class asked the parents what they wanted to learn from the classes. This included the usual labour, pain relief, feeding, caring for baby. All the couples wanted to learn about what equipment they needed for a baby and one of them asked if we could go to the baby shops together and have a look round to see what was really necessary.

I agreed to do this and we made a plan to meet at the Shopping Centre to do this.

The day arrived and eight couples and I went into a baby care shop to have a look around. We looked at lots of equipment and then went to the products shelves.

We were looking at all the different products and they were saying what they thought they needed and then we discussed it.

They each had a basket, which they had filled with what they thought was necessary. They then asked me what I would put in a basket?

I put in cotton wool, muslin nappies, nappies and a bar of baby soap. My basket came to about £19. The heaviest basket came to £106. We were discussing this, when a member of staff came across to us and asked what we were doing?

I had a chat with her and a few minutes later, a manager came over and we were escorted to the door. Apparently, I had encouraged my couples to just buy the basics and they were not happy.

We all went out and were laughing about the situation. I told them that it was easy to go overboard with buying things for the baby, but it wasn't necessary to use all the lotions and potions. Babies were fine with water for the first weeks of their lives, then if they wanted to, they could use different things that they thought they needed.

Needless to say, this was the first and last time I escorted couples on a shopping trip.

# Shocking Wind

I was called into the hospital one evening as they were busy and needed help. When I arrived, I was asked to look after a lady having her first baby who had just had an epidural sited.

I went into the room, introduced myself and talked to the couple about their pregnancy and what they wanted for the delivery.

They were a fun-loving couple and we were soon laughing at the husband's explanations of how his pregnant wife had suffered from terrible flatulence whilst being pregnant and how he was longing for the baby to be born so that this affliction would be over.

It was a rule in our hospital that if a lady had an epidural in place, the midwife should stay in the room at all times. This made sure the lady and her baby were continuing to be happy during her labour and no problems arose. It also gave you time to get to know the parents and encourage them to be prepared for the arrival of their baby.

The lady was doing very well and the signs were showing that the baby would be delivered within the next couple of hours.

A short time later, the lady told me she felt a bit different down below, so I checked and she was fully dilated and ready to push.

I told her we could leave her for a while, before she pushed so that the baby could make its way down the birth canal.

She agreed with this and so we continued for another half an hour and then she felt an urge to push. I told her to do what her body was telling her to do and push with contractions. She was still fairly numb from the epidural, but was managing to push very well with our encouragement.

It became obvious after a short time that the baby was not happy with the pushing, its heartbeat was dropping and taking some time to recover, so I discussed this with the couple then rang the bell and asked for a doctor to come in to assess her.

A 'Registrar' came into the room and agreed that the lady needed some help to deliver. A plan was made that a ventouse (suction) delivery would be the ideal thing to deliver the baby, as the lady had managed to push the baby quite a way down the birth canal. We discussed this with the parents and then I explained that we would put the lady into stirrups, to enable the registrar to deliver the baby.

A colleague came into the room and helped me position her and all of a sudden, as we were raising her legs she farted, long and loud. I was laughing, the other midwife was also laughing and the registrar looked completely shocked. It was hilarious.

The husband just said that's my wife. Windy to the end.

Fortunately, the baby was delivered soon after this and all was well. The Registrar was able to leave the room and we all had a good laugh about the lady's wind.

I cleared up the room, wrote my notes and was able to leave to go home to my bed.

# Post-Natal Depression in Men

I was visiting a lady at home who had had her first baby. She was doing well and the baby was feeding beautifully. Her husband was at home with her and he was finding it all a bit overwhelming.

The husband went into the kitchen to make a cup of tea and the lady told me that she was worried about him as he was very tense and not sleeping. I asked her if she wanted me to have a word with him and she thought this was a good idea.

We carried on chatting and the husband came in with a cup of tea for us. I asked him how he was and he was quite open and saying he was not coping with all the changes and had not slept properly since the baby had been born, as he was so frightened something would happen to his wife or his baby. I asked him if he had ever been depressed and he told me as a teenager, he had been treated for depression when his mother had his youngest brother and was extremely ill after his birth.

I tried to reassure him that his wife was well and the baby was doing fine. I could see that this was not helping so I asked him how he felt about making a doctor's appointment to see if he needed further help.

He was a bit reluctant to do this, but I told him that dads also got postnatal depression and he wasn't anything out of the ordinary and it was nothing to be ashamed of.

I left them to talk about it and agreed to visit the next day.

I visited the next day and was delighted, when the husband told me he had seen his GP the day before and he had been very helpful. He had offered him counselling and medication. The couple had a long talk about what would be right for him and decided to go with medication immediately and counselling later.

I was so pleased that they were moving forward and accepting that they needed help. This was a very brave thing to do and I wish them all the best in their future.

As a footnote, I saw this family about a month later and was delighted that the husband was feeling much more relaxed and was continuing with the anti-depressants. The main point of this was that he was enjoying his baby and had even managed to go back to work. Good for him.

# Surprise Early Delivery

I was visiting a couple who had just been discharged from the maternity unit with their baby. They were a lovely couple, who had been taken by surprise by the arrival of their baby three weeks before the due date. They had been visiting her parents at the time, so had delivered at a different hospital.

The birth had gone well and the baby was a good weight, so they had not had to stay away from home for too long.

The lady was telling me that as she hadn't had her delivery bag with her, she had sent her husband out to get her some shopping such as comfortable knickers, maternity pads, feeding bra and clothes for the baby.

The husband had been diligent in his attempts to fulfil the brief.

They made me laugh about the knickers he had bought. He had been to a shop and bought her thongs. The maternity pads were incontinent pads and the feeding bra was a little lacy number which would not go near her very full breasts.

It was going to take a while for him to live this one down.

The other thing that was funny was that during labour, the wife was paranoid that she would poo herself. Apparently, the husband's answer to this was well, shit happens. According to the lady, the whole of the labour ward were amused by his comment.

It was lovely to see them so happy with their baby and able to laugh about what had happened. They had a really lovely relationship which was great to see.

# Garden Birth

In my capacity as a Supervisor of Midwives, I was asked to go to visit a lady who was requesting a home birth. She lived in a small village and was asking to deliver in her garden.

I arrived at her house and was invited in. The lady was quite young and was expecting her first baby. We discussed how her pregnancy was progressing and what she wanted from her delivery?

She told me that she wanted to deliver in her garden, so that she could commune with nature. I asked her what she meant by this and was informed she liked to wee in the garden as this made her feel free.

I asked to see her garden and was surprised to see that her garden was very overgrown with stinging nettles and was able to be observed by neighbours on both sides.

I told her that it would be really difficult to deliver in the garden as there was no safe place for her to do this. The nettles were at least four feet high and as she had a dog that ran loose in the garden, this would be very unhygienic.

We returned to the house and I discussed her options with her. She was a single mother so I was not happy with her delivering at home, if she had no support for the delivery and postnatal period.

I left her to think about her options and heard later that she had agreed to begin her labour at her home and then transfer to hospital for the delivery, returning home when she was ready.

A plan was made with the community midwives so that the person who was on call at the time she went into labour, she would support her throughout.

The time was nearing when this lady was due and who was on call when the phone message came through. It was me.

I arrived at the lady's house and she was having good contractions. I checked her over and all was well. The baby was happy and the contractions were coming quite quickly.

The lady had promised that she would have a friend with her when she laboured, who would transport her to the hospital and she arrived whilst I was there. The problem was she had arrived on a motor bike. The plan had been that she would drive her to hospital, but I was not happy for her to ride on the back of a bike.

I decided to call an ambulance so that she could be transferred safely to the 'Delivery Suite'.

Fortunately, we had picked an evening when the ambulance service could help us out and the lady was safely transferred.

I met her at the hospital and she actually did very well. Her labour progressed quite quickly and she decided to deliver in the hospital pool. She delivered a beautiful baby boy, who she called Storm.

She had decided that she wanted a Lotus delivery of the placenta. This meant that the cord would not be cut and the placenta would be left with the cord attached until the cord fell off.

I have heard of this before but never seen it happen. I was intrigued to see how this would pan out.

She decided to stay in hospital overnight and returned home the next day.

I was assigned to do her postnatal visits and was intrigued to see what was happening with the cord.

The lady and the baby were doing well, feeding was going well and fortunately, the lady had her friend there to support her. The cord was slowly drying out and the placenta was quite smelly. I had heard that people who have a lotus birth preserved it with lavender and salt. This lady just wanted to leave it alone until it dropped off. I discussed with her that the placenta was actually rotting flesh and would continue to degrade and the smell would probably get worse.

The lady decided to go her own way and leave the placenta alone. I was genuinely worried that this would cause a problem with an infection tracking into the baby. I decided to discuss this with the ladies GP.

The GP was astounded when I spoke to him about the situation, he had never heard of it before. He told me he would visit the lady and have a word with her.

The GP visited the lady and then rang me. He told me the lady had declined his advice and was going to leave the placenta alone. He had informed her that there was a risk of the baby acquiring an infection if things were left.

I visited this lady a few days later and the stench in the house was fairly awful. The placenta had turned green by this point.

I examined the baby and was concerned that the cord area was extremely red and inflamed. The baby was still feeding well but I was concerned the baby would become ill if things were left as they were. Fortunately, the baby appeared well, his temperature was normal at this time but I wondered how long this would last?

I discussed this with the lady and thankfully, she could see that was not in the baby's best interest and allowed me to cut the cord. The problem was what to do with the placenta. Thankfully, the lady agreed to bury it in her garden. I was extremely thankful as I did not want that placenta anywhere near my car.

I rang the GP and explained what had happened and I told him I had taken a swab from the umbilical area as it was red and sore looking. The GP was pleased with the outcome and agreed to give her a prescription for antibiotic powder to put around the cord area.

I visited the lady a few days later and thank goodness, the cord was off and the skin was not red any more. The lady was telling me that next time she had a baby she would do the same thing, but she would use lavender and salt to preserve the placenta.

I was happy to discharge the lady and the baby from our care as she was doing so well. The lady kindly gave me a bunch of daisies and buttercups from her garden to thank me for my help.

Unfortunately, by the time I arrived home the little bunch of flowers were dead. The thought was there and it was very sweet of her to think of me, but I should have put them in water whilst I was doing my clinic.

# Blooming Doulas

I was called out to a home birth to a lady having her first baby. This lady had decided that she did not want any vaginal examinations throughout her labour. This could cause problems as it is difficult to assess progress without this.

I was introduced to her husband and her doula. My heart always sinks when I meet a doula. Some are great and don't interfere with midwives, but others are very vocal and I hoped that this one was easy to get along with. (A doula is a mother's helper. They are not medically trained but have attended a course on childbirth.)

I discussed what was going on with her labour and it transpired she was having contractions every three minutes and they were lasting thirty seconds. The baby's heartbeat was normal and the ladies blood pressure, pulse and temperature were all within normal limits.

I asked her about examining her and she told me in no uncertain terms, that she did not want any intervention at all.

I obliged and watched closely for any progress. The lady continued to contract regularly and appeared to be progressing.

Sometime later, she decided that she wanted to push so I called the second midwife and informed labour ward as to what was happening.

I got ready for the delivery but was not convinced that the lady was ready to push. The baby's head was still quite high and did not appear to be progressing into the pelvis.

The second midwife arrived and I managed to meet her at the door and inform her of what was happening. She groaned and I groaned with her.

We went into the lady's bedroom and I decided to have a chat with her about her progress. I informed her that it was not a good idea to push on a cervix, which was not fully dilated. The doula at this point informed us that they had agreed not to be examined and they were not going back on this. She told the lady not to listen to us as she knew what was best for her.

After swallowing hard and containing my feelings, I told her that we were experienced midwives who wanted what was best for the lady and her baby.

Apparently, this doula had taken a course on how to manage a labour and felt she knew better than all of us how to handle a birth. A very frustrating situation.

We decided to watch and wait. Sometime later the lady started to get distressed and was asking for pain relief. I asked the lady if she would let us examine her as we didn't want to give her pain relief too soon or indeed too late.

I talked to the lady and her husband and told them to discuss it and let us know what they wanted to do.

The doula was very vocal in her wrath of this idea. We were told we were not sticking to the lady's birth plan and we were being unfair.

I told the doula that this was the lady's first baby and it was important to know how the labour was progressing as we didn't want the lady or the baby to become distressed.

The lady came back into the room with her husband and told us she would be examined as she was feeling that she needed pain relief. I suggested that we do that as soon as possible so that we could plan her care.

I examined the lady and unfortunately, she was only 3 cm dilated. The doula informed me that I had obviously made a mistake as the lady wanted to push and she started to tell the lady to do this.

I thought there was going to be a fight. I spoke to the lady and her husband and told her not to push as this would lengthen her labour as her cervix would swell with her pushing on it and take longer for her to get to full dilatation.

Fortunately, at this point the lady told us she wanted an epidural and wanted it as soon as possible. I was quite happy with this and asked my colleague to ring the delivery suite and phone for an ambulance.

The outcome of this birth was that the lady was transferred into the hospital, she was given an epidural and the doula was asked to leave the hospital as she was causing problems. She had argued with the doctors, the midwives and also the couple.

The lady had a twelve-hour labour and unfortunately, had to go to theatre for a section as the baby was not able to navigate the birth canal. The baby was 9 lbs and was found to have its arm over its head which is probably why it was difficult to deliver.

Fortunately, the lady and her husband were happy with the care they had received and apologised to the staff about what had happened with her doula.

I visited this lady when she got home and she was very happy with her care and her baby and thanked me for giving her the chance to labour at home. I was just pleased that it had ended with a happy mum and a healthy baby.

# Different Shoes

I had had a really busy week. I had been called out the night before and was having to run my ante natal class as there was nobody to relieve me.

I set out about 6.30pm, feeling really tired but managed to get the room ready in time to greet my ladies and their partners.

The class was going well when I looked down at my feet and saw that I had odd shoes on. One black, one navy.

I thought it was best to come clean with the group so I told them what I had just found out. I reassured them that I was not barmy, just tired. Thankfully, they saw the funny side of it and the class went well.

The topic for the evening was Labour, pain relief and delivery. We went through the course of labour, telling them what they could do to help themselves. We talked about birth plans, pain relief and the signs of labour.

After we had had a cup of tea, we went over topics that needed more explanation and questions that the group had.

We had the usual questions like how will I know I am in labour. We also had one man wanting to know where the nearest pub was.

The best question was after we had talked about starting labour off. We talked about the normal things, exercise, sex and being offered a stretch and sweep by their midwife or doctor. One of the husbands wanted to know if he could do a scratch and stretch for his wife.

I talked to him about the stretch and sweep and told him that a slap and tickle by him would probably help more than a scratch and stretch. I always smiled after this class whenever I talked about a stretch and sweep. I think his name for it was priceless.

# Sleepy Baby

I was called out one evening to a lady who was worried about her baby. The baby was apparently not feeding well and was very sleepy. I drove to the house and was greeted at the door by a man who invited me in.

I went into the lounge where the lady was sitting with her baby. The baby was sleeping and I asked if I could examine him. I washed my hands and then took the baby. I couldn't help but notice the smell in the house. It was very different to anything I had smelt before.

The state of the house was awful. There were no carpets on the floor, the settee had seen better days and the place was filthy.

I examined the baby asking questions as I went. It appeared the baby had not fed at all for the last 12 hours. The baby had not had a bowel movement or a wet nappy throughout the day. He was definitely sleepy and jaundiced. Jaundice makes the babies skin turn yellow and it can make them very drowsy and difficult to feed. It can also make the baby very ill if not treated. I asked if I could take a blood sample from the baby to test its jaundice levels and permission was given.

The blood sample was obtained and I informed the parents that I would take the blood sample to the hospital and they would be informed of the result. I told them the baby might need admitting to hospital for treatment.

Leaving the house, I went to my car and started to feel really weird. I felt dizzy and my legs and arms felt a bit numb and it was a scary moment.

I made the decision to drive a short distance down the road away from the house, sit for a while to see how I felt.

I was sitting in my car with my head resting on the headrest, when there was a knock on the window. A policeman stood there asking me if I was OK. I had a conversation with the policeman and told them I had just visited a house up the road and was feeling a bit weird. He asked me which house I had visited and when I told him, he told me that it was a drug house and the smell was cannabis.

I was shocked but knew that obviously drugs were available on the estate. The police were very reassuring and told me that I had obviously inhaled cannabis and would feel better very soon but not to drive until I did.

Soon after this, I was able to drive to the hospital with the blood sample and talked to the midwife in charge of the unit. I was obviously concerned about the way the family were living and the safety of the baby. Fortunately for me, the bloods came back showing that the baby needed to come into the hospital for photo therapy to reduce the jaundice levels.

I rang the parents and they agreed to come into the unit. I was very relieved by this and talked to the paediatrician about the baby and the problems I had found in the house.

It was agreed that whilst the baby was in the unit, the mother would be asked questions about the condition of the living conditions and the child protection team would be involved. I was relieved by all this and after updating my notes, I left the unit to go home to my bed.

The outcome to this was that the lady was given help with caring for her baby and was told that she could not take her baby home whilst there were drugs in the house.

It turned out that the father had started cultivating cannabis plants in his attic and after I had left the area, the police had raided the house and found and removed the plants. Apparently, the man had told them it was his only source of income as he couldn't get a job. Unbelievable.

The lady was allowed home with her baby after a few days and was closely monitored by her midwife, health visitor and the child protection team.

# High Blood Pressure

One of my lovely ladies had been admitted by me from my clinic with very high blood pressure. All babies are precious but this lady and her husband had been trying to get pregnant for six years, so of course, they were extremely anxious.

I visited her on the ante natal ward the next morning and she was doing well but seemed a bit down. I sat down to talk to her and she told me that one of the women in the ward was expecting twins and had been told to stay on her bed to give her babies a chance to grow. My lady told me that she was never in her bed and was always leaving the ward to have a cigarette.

I tried to explain to her that everyone was different and she could not be worrying about other people in the ward, she needed to see to her own needs and stop worrying about other people.

I could see that she was very distressed about the situation and spoke to the staff about it. It turned out that the woman concerned was only 27 weeks pregnant and had been admitted because her babies were small and she needed to stay in for rest. Unfortunately, the staff had been unable to keep the lady in her bed. She was forever getting out of the ward and had twice absconded from the hospital to meet her friends in the local pub. Words fail me. This is so unfair to the staff and also to her babies. The staff were spending time several hours a day to get the woman back into the ward.

I went back to my lady and from my conversation with the staff, they had decided that my lady would be better if she was moved to a side room so that her stress levels were lowered. I visited my lady the next day and she was calmer and her blood pressure was under control. It was decided that she could go home and rest at home and she would have her blood pressure checked three times a week.

I heard later that week that the lady who had been giving the staff a headache had delivered and the babies were extremely small for dates and were in the special care baby unit.

Thankfully, my lady went on to deliver her baby normally and her blood pressure settled soon after. I never informed her about the other lady's outcome.

# Language Problems

I was visiting a couple for another midwife. This lady was 34 weeks pregnant and was having problems with her blood pressure, so it was being checked on a regular basis.

I was welcomed in and soon realised that I was going to have a problem with the language barrier. The lady was Italian and her English was not good. Her husband was with her so he could help me out a little. I soon realised his English was not brilliant.

The only answer the lady was saying to my questions sounded like my poor pussy. I was a bit bemused by this and turned to the husband for clarity and he just shrugged his shoulders.

Fortunately, the blood pressure was within normal limits, I told them that someone would come again in two days later to recheck. The lady was still repeating over and over my poor pussy, so I decided to ring the hospital to see if our Italian midwife was on duty and could help me out with translating.

Fortunately, this midwife was on duty and came to the phone. I explained to her what the lady was saying and she said it didn't mean anything to her in Italian but she agreed to talk to the lady so I gave her my phone.

After a short time, the lady handed me my phone back and the midwife told me the lady was telling me that her fanny hurt. Oh dear. I asked the midwife to tell the lady I was happy to look at it for her and this was agreed.

This poor lady had awful haemorrhoids (piles). I arranged to ring her GP to ask for some cream for her to apply to the affected area.

I thanked the midwife who was laughing at the other end of the phone, telling me I should brush up on the names people called their parts.

I must admit I felt a bit of a twerp, but the lady seemed pleased I had got her a prescription to improve her poor pussy. I also gave the girls in the office a good laugh the next morning.

# Pelvis Problems

I went to visit a lady of mine on the ward when she had delivered her baby. She had had a difficult delivery and was feeling a bit sorry for herself. Her baby had been bigger than she thought at 8 lbs 7 ozs and had been helped into the world with forceps.

I gave her a hug and reassured her that she would be feeling better very soon and able to enjoy her baby. I was soon aware that she was really struggling to stand and walk and was in a lot of pain.

I spoke to the staff on the ward asking them to make sure she was seen by a doctor, as I thought she may have separation of the symphysis pubis bone. This is the bone that holds the pelvis together at the front and in some cases can be separated at delivery. It is a very painful condition and can be very debilitating and extremely painful. Fortunately, it is rare for this to happen.

I heard later that morning that she had unfortunately been diagnosed with this condition, and had been given crutches to help her get about.

This is a real problem for someone who has just had a baby, they find it difficult to lift their baby and it is impossible to carry a baby using crutches.

I had found in the past that ladies who are unfortunate enough to have this condition, can become quite depressed which is understandable. I chatted to her and her husband about help when she got home and fortunately, her husband had two weeks off work and following that they thought their mothers would help out.

This lady was very fortunate to live in a house where they had room to have a bed downstairs for her. This condition is extremely debilitating and getting up and down the stairs is extremely painful. Her husband and family did a fantastic job supporting her, but it was nearly six weeks before she was able to walk properly and without pain.

# Challenging Times

My lovely niece Alice was pregnant. She already had a daughter named Edie but had a very difficult birth, long painful and traumatic and she had to have a caesarean to deliver her baby. This was a very traumatic time for her and her husband Tom, who after she had her first baby was told she should have a caesarean if she had another baby. This was a comfort to her as she felt she could not go through another labour like her first one.

Unfortunately, during her $2^{nd}$ pregnancy, she saw a new consultant. When Alice was at 28 weeks of pregnancy, she was told that she could not have the operation but would be expected to have a trial of labour. This means that she would be given time to see how the delivery is going.

As you can imagine, this was not what either Alice or Tom wanted to hear. I had a long chat with them and told them I couldn't do anything as she was not booked to have her baby at the hospital where I worked.

I told them that I would be happy to speak to one of the consultants at our hospital, but it would mean she would have to change hospitals.

They decided that they wanted to do this, so I spoke to a consultant who agreed to see them.

An appointment was made and thankfully, they were told that it would be a mistake for her to try to deliver vaginally and she was offered a caesarean section. Her notes had been acquired from her previous hospital, so they could read how the labour and delivery had gone. A date was given and I had a very happy niece.

I told Alice and Tom that they should inform her hospital that she was no longer going to deliver there and tell them why.

I found out in a phone call from the first hospital when I phoned them that they were trying to cut down on their operative deliveries and this is why she had been declined a caesarean. They were trying to save money. Wow. I was just pleased she was happy.

On the day of the delivery I went into the theatre with Alice whilst she had her epidural sited. I then left so she and Tom could be together. I was lucky enough to see the baby boy Henry soon after his birth. He was gorgeous and thankfully mum and baby did very well.

I know that hospitals need to save money, but I do sometimes wonder how they go about it. A lady's mental state is as important as her physical health. I have had to speak to many women, who were concerned re information they were given that they felt was due to cost cuts. This causes a lot of stress to women and their families.

# Noisy Birth

I was sent to a home birth in a block of flats. The couple lived on the top floor and the lift was out of order. I rang the husband and asked if he could help with the equipment. His reply was sorry I am watching the football.

Well thanks for that. I was exhausted by the time I got to the top floor. I had a huge delivery bag, my ante natal bag and the gas and air. I arrived at the flat to hear quite a lot of screaming. This was going to be a noisy birth.

I introduced myself and went into the flat. The lady was sitting on the sofa shouting with each contraction and the husband was cheering on his team. The louder the lady shouted, the louder the television became. My head was pounding and I had only just got there.

I took the lady into her bedroom to talk to her and to assess her progress. This was her second baby and she had had a very normal pregnancy and wanted to deliver at home, so her other child wouldn't be disturbed.

I must admit I was surprised the child was still asleep. The noise in the flat was awful.

The lady was doing very well and all her observations were within normal limits. The lady had several contractions whilst I was in the bedroom with her and screeched with each one. I was informed that by shouting she was easing her pain. Well if that rocked your boat, I would have to put up with it.

This lady did very well and was progressing quite quickly. I called the second midwife and heaved a sigh of relief that the football was over and the television was turned off. Now, I just had to contend with the lady's noise.

All of a sudden, there was a knock at the door and I was thinking it was the midwife. The husband went to the door and in walked two policemen. A neighbour had phoned the police thinking someone in the flat was being murdered. I laughed and told them to wait a minute until another contraction came.

The policemen were visibly shocked by the noise the lady was making and told her she was causing a noise and upsetting the neighbours. I can't possibly write in full what she replied but it was very colourful and basically, she told them what she had told me, it helped her cope with the pain. I was waiting for their reply but they just said we will inform the neighbour that all is well and that hopefully the noise will stop soon. I was with them; my head was pounding.

At that moment, the second midwife arrived and must have wondered what on earth was going on? Thankfully at that moment, the lady said she wanted to push. I spoke to the policemen and said hopefully when she is concentrating on pushing, she won't have the time or inclination to shout.

How wrong I was. Now we had another problem. Her son had woken up and was also crying. I felt like joining in. I asked the husband to take the little boy back into his bedroom and try to placate him. I spoke to the woman and asked her to try to keep the noise down to a minimum.

The police left at this point and thankfully, the lady started to push.

Shortly after this, the baby arrived and the peace was lovely, just the sound of the baby crying. It was utter bliss. The neighbours were obviously delighted that the noise had stopped, as were my ears. We cleared up the room and after a shower, tucked the lady up in bed and made ready to leave.

I again asked the husband for help with the equipment to be informed he was exhausted and was going to bed. Well that's okay then, thanks for that.

# Strange Goings On

When I first started on community in Milton Keynes, I had a patient who seemed to be having an awful lot of problems with her first pregnancy.

She was complaining of pain and bleeding from very early on in her pregnancy. I sent her to the hospital on many occasions, but she was always discharged fairly readily each time.

When she reached 28 weeks pregnancy, I was called once again for pain and bleeding, I had to once again admit her to the hospital. The hospital kept her in this time and I went back to work.

The following day, I had a phone call asking if I could attend the hospital to discuss this patient's care. As she was in a hospital out of my normal area, I rang my manager and was given permission to go and see them about this lady.

I arrived at the hospital and was taken into the sisters office and I was told that they had reason to believe that this lady was making herself bleed by performing examinations on herself. I must admit I was a bit gob smacked and lost for words. Apparently, a midwife had walked into this lady's room when she was examining herself.

It was a really difficult situation. I asked if anyone had broached the subject with the lady and if so, what was her reaction?

A senior midwife had spoken to the lady and she had become very distressed denying that this was what was happening. The lady had been told that she was to be discharged from hospital that day and they would only see her again when she was in labour, unless she had a real problem.

I thought it best that I didn't inform the lady that I knew what she was being accused of, so I didn't go and see her at this point.

When I got back into my own area, I went into the surgery and spoke to the ladies GP, who was shocked to hear what had been apparently happening.

This lady was a frequent patient at the surgery and the GP thought that because the ladies husband worked away from home, she was left alone for long periods. He agreed with me that we would have to support this lady as much as we could without condemning her for what she had apparently been doing.

I visited this lady at home the next day and nothing was said by me, but she told me what the hospital had said to her. I told her I was there to support her and her unborn baby and I would do my best to do this. I told her to put from her mind what had happened and start again from a clean slate.

The outcome of this story is that the lady delivered at 38 weeks of pregnancy, she never again throughout the rest of her pregnancy called me to say she was in pain or bleeding. She was given extra support from the health visitor and myself and did really well. They moved soon after the birth so that she had more support from her family whilst her husband was working away.

# Another On-Call, Another Birth

I was second on call and was called at 02:00 hours, to attend a delivery on an estate some miles from where I lived.

When I arrived, I was greeted by the midwife, husband and the lady. She had been labouring for some hours and was currently 7 cm. The lady coped very well with her contractions and was mobilising throughout this time.

We had been there some time when the lady told us she wanted to push. We prepared for the birth but I was a bit dubious this was going to happen at home as the lady was becoming very distressed and asking for pain relief. She was given gas and air but this bought no relief, so I suggested that the lady should be examined to ascertain if she could be given an injection of Pethidine or whether it was too late to give to her. We don't like to give this injection too late as if the baby is born within an hour, it can make the baby sleepy and sometimes they have difficulty coping with the birth and are slow to respond once born.

The other midwife examined her and suddenly announced that she thought the baby was breech and that the lady was fully dilated. I was asked by the midwife if I would check this and after talking to the lady and getting her permission, I examined her.

The baby was not breech. It was presenting by its face which means that the lady needed to be transferred into the hospital as the baby could not be delivered in this position. I talked to the lady and her husband, who agreed to go in and an ambulance was called.

I went in the ambulance with the lady and advised her not to push as this would not do her or her baby any good. The baby's face would become swollen and it could make the delivery more difficult.

This lady was great, she was so calm and composed and was taken into the labour ward, where a team of doctors and midwives were waiting for her.

Most face presentation deliveries end up in a Caesarean but this lady was so compliant, the registrar was able to deflect the baby's head and the lady pushed her baby out on her own. The babies face was quite bruised but came to no harm and the lady and her husband were thrilled with the outcome.

The other midwife felt bad for thinking it was breech, but as I said to her what she thought was the baby's anus was actually its mouth, it's not an easy situation to be in but these things happen. The lady would have been transferred in with a breech baby so the outcome would have been the same.

# A Call Out to the Delivery Suite

I was called in to work on the unit as they were really busy. I answered the phone as there was no one around and a husband was telling me his wife's waters had broken so they were coming in. I replied we would see them when they arrived.

Later that evening, I was flitting from room to room helping out where I could, when there was someone ringing the bell to the delivery suite. I answered the bell and the husband I had spoken to earlier arrived at the desk. I asked him where his wife was and he informed me he had left her at home as he didn't want her to have a wasted journey. Incredibly, he handed me a jam jar with his wife's amniotic fluid inside.

Trying to keep a straight face, I told him that his wife needed to attend in person as we could not check her to see all was well if she was at home. The midwife who had been at the desk with me quickly scarpered as she was trying hard not to laugh.

I asked him if he would go home and fetch his wife so that we could make sure all was well with her and her baby. Thankfully, he agreed and left me holding the jam jar much to the amusement of the other midwives around me.

Sometime later, the couple arrived and all was well with mum and baby. She was admitted to the ward as she was 37 weeks pregnant, having some contractions but was not yet in established labour.

I was asked to look after a lady who had just arrived on the delivery suite who was in established labour. I entered her room and introduced myself. This lady was having her first baby and was coping really well.

I was looking through her notes and saw she was 5 ft 1 in tall and had measured normally throughout her pregnancy. I examined her abdomen with her permission and thought she was having quite a large baby. I obviously didn't want to alarm the lady, so I asked her if she had ever been told during her pregnancy that she was having a good-sized baby. Her answer was, no my midwife thinks it will be about 5 or 6 lbs.

I beg to differ but kept that to myself. Her husband was 6 ft 4 in, so I told her that her baby felt very long and I thought her baby was a bit bigger than 6 lbs. I thought to myself it was more like 8 or 9 lbs or even bigger.

As she and the baby were doing so well, I encouraged her to mobilize and breathe through her contractions and went to the desk outside to speak to one of the other midwives.

I informed the senior midwife that I thought the baby felt quite large but as the mum was doing so well, we would watch and wait.

This lady was so controlled it was so nice to see. Her husband was great and was supporting her through each contraction.

Sometime later, the lady felt the urge to push so she got herself positioned on all fours on the bed and I encouraged her to do what her body was telling her to do.

I also informed her and her husband that I would be asking another midwife to attend the birth, so that there was another pair of hands to help her and her baby. I didn't tell her I thought we may run into problems if the baby was as big as I thought.

Well how wrong I was. This lady was an absolute star, she did exactly as I asked and a rather large head was delivered followed by a very long body. I passed the baby to the parents, who were surprised at the size but delighted with their lovely baby.

I was asked to weigh the baby before they rang their parents. I did this and was quite shocked when the baby weighed in at 10 lbs 6 oz. The lady had no stitches and had coped beautifully.

The parents quizzed me on how big I thought the baby would be and I told them I thought the baby would be 8 or 9 lbs, so I was shocked at how well she had done. They did wonder why the size of the baby had not been diagnosed during her pregnancy. Not a question I could answer, but as I told them it was irrelevant as she had done so well. I did say that if she had been diagnosed earlier with a large baby, she would have been referred to a consultant who may had asked her to be induced on or before her due date in case she ran into problems, so overall it had turned out very well.

This lady was so happy with her birth and her baby. She sat in her bed breastfeeding her baby and looked so beautiful. I cleared the room up and said my goodbyes and was able to go home to my bed.

# Missed Appointments

Another day dawned and my clinic was in full flow. I felt very fortunate to work in a surgery, where most of the ladies turned up for their appointments. It was very seldom I had to chase women up who missed appointments. It looked as if my luck was going to run out.

I had inherited a lady from another area, who was forgetting her appointments on a regular basis. I contacted this lady on a regular basis and she promised to come to the next clinic. Unfortunately, this did not happen so I rang her and offered to see her at home at the weekend. This was accepted.

I arrived at the lady's house and the ante natal check was done. I talked to her about the importance of attending her appointments. I was informed that she had a very important job and it was very difficult to take time off to attend the surgery. I also told her she was entitled to time off to attend her appointments.

This is a really difficult situation to be in, it was important to make sure this lady was seen regularly so I suggested that I saw her at home on the weekends, I was working to make this easier for her. This was taken up and thankfully, this worked out for her and for me. I did suggest that once she was on maternity leave, she should come to the surgery. This was agreed and thankfully this worked out well.

This lady worked until she was 38 weeks pregnant and delivered a week later. I visited her at home and she told me she wished she had left work earlier as she had not had time to rest at all.

Ladies who have high pressured jobs, sometimes find it hard to leave with enough time to prepare for their babies. Most women who work up until the birth, find this hard and if they go on to have other babies, they leave earlier.

# Big Breasts

I was visiting a lady who was having problems breastfeeding. I did not know this lady but had been informed by a colleague that she had rather large breasts.

I arrived at the house and was invited in. The lady was sitting on the couch with her baby, so I introduced myself and we had a chat about the difficulties she was having. It was her wish that we go up to her bedroom to feed her baby as she had relatives staying.

I suggested the lady made herself comfortable and I would help her with the feeding. The lady told me she would get changed ready to feed and I went into the bathroom to wash my hands. I went straight into the bedroom and found the lady sitting on the bed with her bra off. Her breasts were enormous. Bless her, I helped her fix her baby on her right breast and to my astonishment she threw her left breast over her shoulder. I must admit I was a little shocked and found it a trifle amusing at the way she was feeding, but fortunately the baby fixed on the breast and fed well. The lady was thrilled and told me that moving her other breast out of the way had been the answer. She told me that before she was pregnant, she wore a 46GG bra. Poor girl, her breasts were so heavy they were causing pain in her shoulders and her back.

This baby fed really well and actually gained weight quite quickly. I saw this lady several days later and she informed me that when she had finished breastfeeding, she was going to ask her GP for a breast reduction. I must admit I have always felt that this being done on the National Health Service (NHS) was a difficult situation but for this lady, I could not see any other way of making her comfortable. I hope she got her wish.

# Dummies

I was visiting a lady of mine who had just had her third baby. It was the middle of the afternoon when I reached her house and she told me her husband had just gone to fetch her two girls from school.

The lady was doing very well and told me all about her birth which had gone as planned. The baby was asleep in its cot so I asked if I could examine it. This was agreed.

I washed my hands and then lifted the baby out of its cot. Whilst I was undressing him, he started to cry and a dummy was given to him by his mother.

The baby was well and was feeding regularly.

Just after this, the husband arrived with the two girls. One was six and the other was almost five. They both had dummies in their mouths. The eldest girl was talking to me but I couldn't understand what she was saying. I asked her to remove her dummy so that I could understand her.

I noticed that both of the girls had very strange teeth, they appeared to have grown into a dummy shape. I had a conversation with the mum about dummies and she told me that they had all had them since they were born and it was the only way of keeping them quiet.

I have no problem with people using dummies, what I don't like to see is a mum shove a dummy in a baby's mouth every time they start to cry. They need to cry, it's their only way of communicating. I also think when children go to school, they need to be dummy free.

# Badly Behaved Teenagers

Some years ago, I was asked to go into a fairly local school to speak to a group of girls who were studying for a Health and Social Care Course. I had never done this before but got together a lot of leaflets, pamphlets plus a uterus that would show a growing baby throughout a pregnancy.

I arrived on the day to be greeted by sixteen girls and three teachers. I introduced myself and asked what the girls wanted from the session.

I was quite shocked when one girl asked if she got pregnant would she get a house? also what benefits could she apply for? Once my chin had lifted off the floor, I replied that it wasn't a given that getting pregnant would provide anybody with a house or indeed benefits.

It became apparent that no one in the class was in the least bit interested in the topic and were extremely badly behaved. They were talking to one another, throwing things across the room and behaving in an unruly fashion.

Not one of the teachers chastised them or intervened. I was very thankful when the session came to an end.

I learnt afterwards that this group of girls were not at all interested in learning and were just looking forward to the day when they could leave school. The teachers had thought they would engage with a midwife, but obviously this did not happen.

Later in the same year, I was asked to attend again. I politely declined.

# Naughty Children

I was doing a clinic for a midwife who was on holiday. The first lady was a booking a first appointment, which takes about an hour.

The lady came in with her son, who was six. He was very inquisitive and was inspecting all the drawers and cupboards. I asked him not to do this as I was worried he would find something that could harm him.

He climbed all over the furniture and was making an awful lot of noise. His mother was very tolerant of him, but I actually found it quite stressful. Suddenly, he asked his mum for a drink and I was quite shocked when she opened her bra and started breastfeeding him. I have no objections to anyone breastfeeding a child in my presence, but this child was actually holding his mother's breast and twisting it in his hands.

The mother told me that he fed first thing in the morning and again in the evening, she had also been known to go to the school at lunch time to satisfy his needs. I must admit I had a picture in my head of the lady arriving to do this and passing her boob through the school's railings.

I was quite relieved when the appointment was over and I could put the room to rights. There was stuff everywhere,

where the boy had taken things out of drawers and cupboards. I began to wonder how this child would be when the baby was born and needed his mum's breasts to feed. I do hope it all worked out for them.

# Young and Pregnant

I was half way through my clinic when I had a phone call from one of the GPs asking me if I could see a new pregnant lady as soon as possible. As I had two appointments free at the end of my clinic due to two ladies delivering, I agreed I could see her then.

This lady came into my room and it was apparent she was quite young. I introduced myself and asked her about her pregnancy. It became known that she was 16 years old and was shocked to find herself pregnant.

We talked about what support she had and whether the baby's father was still in the picture. She told me that her parents did not know she was pregnant or that she had a boyfriend.

This girl was a lovely intelligent teenager who after discussion decided to talk to her parents and her boyfriend about the situation and then let me know if she wanted to continue with the pregnancy.

The dates that she was able to give me showed that she was 11 weeks pregnant, so I urged her to do this as soon as possible as if she did want to terminate the pregnancy, she only had a week left to decide and then to go through the procedure.

I reassured her that it was her body and her pregnancy and of course, what she had told me would stay with me and would not be discussed with anyone outside the surgery.

I gave the girl my telephone number and told her that if she wanted to discuss anything at any time, she could ring me.

The girl phoned me the next day and told me that after talking to her parents and boyfriend, she had decided to keep the baby and had the support of everyone.

I arranged to see her at her parent's house the following weekend.

I arrived at the girl's house and was invited in by her father. They were a lovely family and although shocked by the news of the pregnancy, were very supportive and would welcome the new baby into the family.

The appointment went well until the topic of blood tests came up. The girl was very apprehensive about having blood taken, but with reassurance coped very well. The girl's father was standing next to her putting a reassuring hand on her shoulder until the blood appeared. Unfortunately, he fainted and slumped to the floor. Fortunately, the girl stayed still and I was able to finish the test.

We then sat the father up against the settee and reassured him that his daughter was fine and that our concern at that time was for him to see if he had hurt himself.

Fortunately, he was fine after a cup of tea, a biscuit, and a sit down.

The girl was talking about who she wanted with her when she gave birth to her child. I wish I could have videoed the father's face when she told him she wanted him and her mother there.

The boyfriend was going to support her as much as he could, but he was still at school so it was a difficult situation. His parents were aware of the pregnancy and had been in contact with the family to assure them they would be supportive.

We then discussed when she should tell the school about her pregnancy. I thought that this was their choice and they had time to think about it as she was still early on in pregnancy.

I asked if she minded being seen by a consultant as she was so young and she agreed and her mother requested my favourite one, so I was quite happy to have a word with him and I knew that he would be very happy to see her.

I arranged to see the girl again after she had had her scan and told them they could ring me at any time and I would be happy to discuss any problems they were having.

I seem to have left a very happy family behind.

The outcome of this pregnancy was that the girl did extremely well. She attended school full-time, until she was 36 weeks and the school was very supportive with giving her work to do at home once she had left. I was also pleased that her friends were supporting her and she had had no harassment from anyone throughout her pregnancy.

She was seen by the consultant, who was really good with her and told her she was very normal and nobody would intervene unless she ran into problems.

The girl went into labour when she was 39 weeks pregnant, she coped with the labour extremely well and gave birth to a beautiful baby girl who weighed 6 lbs 8 oz. She had her parents and her boyfriend with her to support her. Her father apparently closed his eyes and sat down when the actual birth happened.

I saw her in the hospital and when she returned home and she was an absolute star with her baby. She was breastfeeding her and coping with the baby's care with the help of her mum and dad.

I was told that when the baby was 6 weeks old, she would be returning to school to continue her education and her mum would be looking after her baby during the day for her. She intended to carry on breastfeeding in the morning before she went to school. She would then feed in the evening and during the night.

This family was superb in their care and support of their daughter and her baby and I recently saw her with her child who is now at school. She had finished her education and been to a local university to do a Teaching Course and was now teaching a fairly local school. The father of the baby and her were now married and she was pregnant with her second baby. It was a great outcome for her and her family and I am so pleased it turned out as it did.

# Private Patients

One weekend, I was asked to visit a lady who had delivered out of area. I knew nothing about her, but from her address knew it was in a lovely area.

I arrived at the house and was invited in. I was informed that the lady who had given birth was having lunch with friends and would not like being interrupted. I told the lady who apparently was the housekeeper that it was unfortunate, but I was unable to return at a different time as I was busy.

The housekeeper went into the dining room and I heard the lady say it's really inconvenient but if she must visit, you can ask her to come in.

I went into the room to be faced with a large table, which was surrounded by about 12 people. I was introduced to the lady and told her I was there to make sure her and her baby were well. I looked around the table and noticed a lady that was from the hospital I worked at and I knew her fairly well, I smiled at her but she completely ignored my presence. The said lady obviously didn't want her friends to know that she knew a mere midwife.

I asked the lady if we could go into another room and have a chat. She huffed and agreed to leave the table and told her guests she would be two minutes.

We went into another large room and I asked if she had any notes for me to look at. I was told firmly that she had but she had not got time to fetch them.

My next question was can I see the baby? I was bluntly told no.

The lady informed me that as a private patient, she expected me to visit at her convenience not mine. I informed her I worked for the National Health Service, so was not a private midwife and unfortunately, it was difficult for me to give an exact appointment time.

The lady considered this, then told me she would prefer a private midwife and would sort this out herself.

I said my goodbyes, leaving her with my mobile number and rang the midwife in charge of the unit to inform her of what had happened. I told her that I would ring the office the next morning to inform them, so that someone could make sure the lady was getting the care and support she needed.

The outcome to this story was that I rang the office on the Monday morning and a midwife rang the lady. She was informed that she was going to London for her postnatal visits, so she was asked to refrain from ringing her and wasting her time. How rude is that? London is a long way to go to make sure all is well for the lady and her baby but obviously, if that is what she wanted to do we would be happy with that.

# Not Happy to Push

One of my ladies, who booked with me was terrified of giving birth vaginally. I was very respectful of this and assured her that I would help her as much as I could. I referred her to a consultant to discuss this.

Throughout this lady's pregnancy, I tried to reassure her about birth. Her consultant appointment had left her feeling a little anxious as at the time, her consultant was not available and she had been told by the registrar that he couldn't make a decision about the birth, until later on in her pregnancy. They had arranged to see her when she was 36 weeks pregnant.

I tried to reassure her that all would be well and that things would turn out as she wished. I tried to get to the bottom of her fears. It turned out her mother had had a very difficult birth and had obviously talked to her daughter about this and frightened the girl to death.

Reassurance that times have changed and that births are different these days was falling on deaf ears.

The lady reached 35 weeks pregnant and at her appointment, I found that her baby was in the breech position. I informed the lady of this and told her that she would be offered a section if the baby stayed in this position. This made the lady very happy and we discussed that when she saw the consultant, she may be offered a procedure to help turn the baby into the right position. I told her that I would organize a scan for her so that we could see what breech position the baby was in.

Some breech babies are in the sitting position with their legs flexed. Some babies are in a position, where their legs are straight so the baby is in a V-position. I told the lady that if the latter was true, it was more difficult to turn the baby.

I had a phone call from this lady the following week telling me her baby was in the open scissor position i.e. feet up by its face, so fortunately she was likely to offered a section.

This made the lady very happy, as I said to her things always turn out for the best.

The outcome was she had a section at 39 weeks of pregnancy and all was well with her and her baby, and they were very happy, very well and relieved that the delivery had gone as she had wished. Phew, that was a relief.

Another lady booked with me and informed me at the first appointment that she was having a section and there was no way she was going to give birth. I asked her about this and she informed me that her bits were hers and she could do as she liked with them. She didn't want the vagina of an old woman by giving birth vaginally. I tried to reassure her that if she did pelvic floor exercises after the birth of her baby, this would not happen.

That went down a storm. She told me that she was going to deliver at a private hospital in London and would be having a section and a tummy tuck at the same time. I asked her if she had any connections with the hospital she was talking about, but she informed me that I needed to sort that out for her.

I arranged for her to meet with a consultant in his private clinic to discuss this. The outcome was she was looked after by this consultant throughout the pregnancy and went in for a section at 38 weeks of pregnancy. This is a little earlier than it would normally have been done but apparently, the lady was fed up of being pregnant so wanted the baby out.

I visited this lady after the birth and she was happy with the delivery and aftercare. She also had arranged for a maternity nurse to be with her at home so that she could rest and recuperate from the birth.

She actually did really well, but told me that she was disappointed that she could not get back into her size 8 jeans. I reassured her that this was really normal and would come with time. I told her that her breastfeeding her baby would help her do this. I was told in no uncertain terms that she was not breastfeeding as her breasts were hers not her baby's. Everyone is different and thinks differently, now I had the answer as to why she looked so well and refreshed, she was not looking after the baby herself, just having a cuddle occasionally. The nurse was feeding the baby during the night and also in the daytime to let the lady rest. Everyone is different and have different needs.

I sometimes wonder why people have babies if they don't appear to look after them alone, but have so much help it's amazing.

# Poo Explosion

I visited a lady of mine that had twins. She and the babies were doing very well with feeding and they were sleeping well.

They were due to have their PKU (Phenylketonuria)blood test, which all babies have on day five. This looks for a lot of things and is offered to all babies.

We went into the nursery to do the blood tests. The lady had a changing unit and then two cots lined up one behind the other on the same wall. The baby in the cot nearest to the changing unit was awake, so we decided to attend to this baby first. I performed the blood test and then stripped the baby off to weigh. I was talking to mum as I was doing this and had just looked her way, when the baby farted and shot poo across the changing mat, his own cot and onto the other twin's face. It was hilarious and the baby lay there with poo dripping down his face fast asleep. We quickly cleaned the poo away and were laughing about how far the poo had travelled.

I explained that breastfed babies poo can travel a long way. I have seen a baby who was laying on a carpet shoot it across the room onto the wall. I have also seen a little boy who was lying on the floor on a rug wee into a cup of tea that was a foot away from him.

You would think that after all the years I have worked as a midwife, I would have learnt my lesson in this department but some babies are just too quick.

# Sick Husband

One of my ladies was having her third baby. She had two boys, who were quite young and was expecting a girl. She was seeing me for her appointment when she was 28 weeks pregnant and was telling me she was worried that her husband was slightly unwell. He was complaining of a headache and some visual problems. I asked if he had seen a doctor and she told me he was reluctant to do so as he didn't want to take time off work.

I told her that she could always have a word with the GP and voice her concerns. As it happened, she needed a prescription from the GP so I asked him to come to the room and have a word with her.

The GP was great, he told her that he obviously couldn't make a diagnosis without seeing him but he would be happy for her husband to see him that same evening, after he got home from work.

I heard later that week that the GP had seen him and sent the husband to the hospital for a scan and unfortunately, he had been diagnosed with a brain tumour.

I rang the lady who told me that her husband was going into hospital the next day for a biopsy and hopefully to have the tumour removed. At this point, it was unknown whether the tumour was benign or not?

Obviously, the lady was extremely worried about all this but was grateful to the doctor who had taken action so quickly.

I told the lady that she should ring and let me know how it went and obviously if I could do anything to help, I would be happy to do this.

After he had surgery, it was found to be cancerous. The tumour was removed and he was to undergo chemotherapy to help mop up any stray cells, and then radiotherapy.

The lady's pregnancy went well, but it was really hard for her as her husband was now unable to work and was very unwell. This was a really difficult position to be in at any time but in late pregnancy with two young children, it was awful.

This lady was seen by a consultant who agreed to induce her at 39 weeks to ensure that her husband was well enough to attend the delivery.

A baby girl was delivered who was perfect and she was brought home the next day by her parents. Her husband was obviously unwell, but was able to bond with his daughter. Unfortunately, he was not up to helping around the house as he was unsteady on his feet but he was able to cuddle the baby and keep the other children amused whilst his wife was busy.

This is a very difficult situation for anyone, but the lady was an absolute star and took it all in her stride. I have the utmost respect for her. Fortunately, she had a supportive family who helped her out as best they could.

This husband was so lovely and was absolutely charming. When I discharged her from my care, I made sure the lady could keep in contact with me for any support that she needed.

Unfortunately, this husband died when the baby was very young. A very difficult position for the lady to be in, to be widowed so young.

I kept in contact with the lady for some time and she did really well. She decided to move area to be nearer her and his parents so that they could support her. I wish her well.

# Gas and Air

One of my ladies was booked for a home birth she had a very normal pregnancy and I was able to attend her delivery.

I was called at 11 pm and arrived to find her in good labour. She was contracting regularly and was mobilizing well. I did all the usual things like blood pressure, pulse, temperature finding they were all within normal limits. The baby's heart beat was also within normal limits.

We had discussed her birth plan whilst she was pregnant and I knew that she wanted no pain relief apart from gas and air.

Shortly after I got to the house, I examined her and found her to be 8 cm dilated. I was able to ask the lady if she wanted to start the gas and air and she agreed that she did.

Then the fun started, she used the equipment to good effect and found the pain relief was really helping her. Each time she used the gas during a contraction, she started laughing, not just a small laugh she gave what I said was a belly laugh, she was also singing. It was hysterical, I was laughing, her husband was laughing and when the contraction had eased and she stopped using it, she wondered what the joke was.

We tried to explain to her what was happening each time she had a contraction but she found it difficult to understand. Her husband decided to film her on his mobile phone to show her why we found it so funny.

She stood up with each contraction, laughed and was also singing at the top of her voice. I have never seen anything like it, it was so amusing. I just encouraged her to carry on as she was because it was obviously working and so it continued.

Shortly after this, I called the second midwife who arrived shortly after. The lady by this point wanted to push so I suggested that she stopped using the gas and concentrated on her pushing. This did not go down very well so I let her continue using it to see how coped.

I have never seen before or since anyone laughing, singing and pushing at the same time. It was very comical but worked for her. All too soon, it was apparent the baby was ready to be born, so reluctantly, I took the gas from her so she could understand what I was telling her.

The baby arrived quite quickly and was handed to mum who was obviously thrilled. Once she had delivered her placenta, her husband showed her the video he had taken of her during the labour. Luckily, she found it amusing but told him she would disown it if he put it on Facebook.

When we had cleaned up and were drinking a lovely cup of tea, the husband asked if he could buy gas and air online so he could get his wife to repeat her antics at any time. Unfortunately, I had to tell him that this was not available to buy but he could always show her the video and they could have a laugh about it.

We left a very happy couple and a beautiful baby to enjoy their lives together.

# Birth After Miscarriage

I booked a lady for pregnancy who was really anxious. She had 2 children but had recently suffered a miscarriage. She had only just moved into my area, so I had not met her before.

I managed to book her in for an early scan to try to set her mind at rest about this pregnancy. I also offered extra appointments so that she felt more reassured. She told me that she had not been happy with the ante natal care she had received with her last baby. I told her I couldn't put that right but we will make sure she was well supported in this pregnancy.

This lady was so anxious that I went to listen in to the heart beat for her on a very regular basis. Towards the latter stages of her pregnancy, this was every week. I got to know her and her family very well. If that's what it takes to make a lady happy, it's fine.

Eventually and after what seemed like a long pregnancy for the lady, she delivered a beautiful baby girl so was obviously very happy as was I.

When you get to know your ladies so well, it is really sad when you discharge them, they feel like part of the family. I was lucky to be able to see some of my ladies as I lived a short distance from where I worked, so could see a lot of my ladies when they were out and about with their babies which was lovely for me. I was also lucky enough to see a lot of my mums and their offspring at the local primary school, where I help on a voluntary basis on a Tuesday and Wednesday.

# Delivering a Midwife

I booked a lady who informed me she was a qualified midwife but did not practise as she felt she could not provide the care to the ladies that she felt they needed.

I promised I would treat her as a pregnant lady and not as a midwife. The booking went well and we discussed where she would like to have her baby. She wanted a home birth so I was happy to go along with this.

This lady had a normal pregnancy and I had promised to be at the birth if I possibly could. Everything was looking good for the birth. She and her husband were excited and we all hoped she would give birth in good time so that she could achieve her home birth.

The call came and fortunately, I was able to attend. It was obviously a night delivery, most of them seem to happen at night. The contractions were regular and she coped really well. It was a long night and we were all tired but she did so well.

The time came to call the second midwife who arrived shortly afterwards. By this time she was 9 cm, so nearly there. I encouraged her to move about and she did this really well. In due course, she was fully dilated and started to push with her contractions.

The pushing stage was coming up to an hour and my colleague was getting anxious and saying she thought that we should think about transferring into the hospital. I was aware of her anxieties, but I said we should give her time as she and the baby were coping very well.

The second stage of labour, the pushing stage usually lasts about an hour with a first time mum, it is usually much quicker in woman who has given birth before.

I could see my colleague was becoming anxious about the time she had been pushing, but I could see that the baby was going to put in an appearance shortly.

Fortunately, my feelings were right and shortly after this, the baby's head was delivered followed quite quickly by the body. A beautiful baby boy who cried lustfully to make his presence known.

The placenta delivered shortly after this and we got mum sat comfortably on her sofa with dad and her son. It was a lovely moment.

The birth had taken 13 hours, so we were all tired but we left a very happy mum, dad and a baby.

This lady went on to have 2 more sons, both of whom I delivered. Her second birth when I got to her, she was telling me she could not cope and needed to go into hospital. I reassured her and 30 mins later her $2^{nd}$ son was delivered much to her surprise.

With her $3^{rd}$ son it happened again. I arrived and sometime later, I believe it was about 15 mins, her baby came into the world.

It is lovely to be able to deliver your own ladies. All births are special but there is something so rewarding about delivering women you have got to know very well.

# Out of Area

I was visiting a lady of mine who lived in the area, but had moved temporarily into a house in a village just outside my area whilst her house was being modernised. I was lucky enough to be able to visit her. She was a lovely lady who was having her second baby. This lady was a good friend of my eldest daughter Charlotte, so she kept me informed of how things were going with this lady's pregnancy.

Shortly before this lady delivered, my beautiful granddaughter Evee was admitted to hospital with an abscess in a salivary gland in her neck. She was only tiny at the time, so it was obviously very distressing for Charlotte and Justin. I visited her regularly and she had to have two operations to drain it, so it was a very anxious time.

The day after Evee's second operation, this lady was home and I was on my way to visit her. I found my way to her house. This lovely lady was having a bad day and was very tearful. We had a cuddle and I reassured her that she was doing really well. Her husband went to make us both a cup of tea and once the lady was reassured that all was well, she asked me how Evee was?

I told her what was happening with her and not long afterwards we were both crying, I was so distressed about

Evee but it was very unprofessional to cry with a patient. Fortunately, the lady was lovely and realised that I was obviously really concerned about what was happening. Nobody wants to see a child go through surgery at all, but when it's someone so close it's very distressing. The state Charlotte was in was also upsetting, so she had a lot of mummy cuddles and I tried to help her as much as I could.

I left shortly afterwards and by this time, we were both smiling and laughing about our little break down. The poor husband wondered what was happening when he came into the room with his tea and saw two weeping women.

Thankfully, the second operation worked and two days later Evee was able to go home and has thankfully never had the problem again. Apparently, it is really rare to have this problem but thanks to a superb GP and the care of the hospital, she was absolutely fine.

# Overanxious Mum

One of my ladies expecting her first baby was really anxious. She was actually doing really well and I tried to alleviate her fears each time I saw her.

When she delivered, I saw her in the hospital and she was coping really well with her baby. Fortunately, she had a normal delivery so was feeling well herself. She told me she was going home that day and that her husband would be with her for two weeks to support her. I told her I would see her at home the next day and left to get on with my day.

I arrived at the ladies house the next day to find that the lady was finding life extremely difficult. Unfortunately, the baby had kept mum and dad up most of the night and they were worried there was something wrong with the baby.

On examining the baby, I reassured the parents that the baby was fine. His colour was good, he was filling his nappy and had just had a wakeful night. I reassured the parents that this was not unusual and that things usually settled down.

I stayed with them and watched the lady feed her baby. The baby feed very well and I helped them wind him and settle him down. I told them to feed him regularly and not to leave him over four hours in the day time. I told them that as he was well and a good-size, they could leave him during the night if he slept for long periods. I arranged for them to receive a visit the next day and told them I would visit them three days later.

When I arrived in the office three days later, I was informed that the lady was still very anxious but the baby was doing very well.

Arriving at the house, it was obvious that the baby was well but the mum was struggling. The poor lady looked exhausted. I gave her a hug and asked her to tell how things were going. It became apparent that the lady was so concerned that something would happen to her baby that she was not going to bed, she was sitting up watching the baby.

Bless her. This is a really difficult situation, the lady was struggling to sleep, she was breastfeeding her baby and not eating properly. I talked to her and her husband and told them that they needed to sleep or they would not enjoy their baby. I reassured them that nothing untoward would happen. The baby was in the same room as them and they would hear him when he needed their attention.

I asked the lady if she would be willing to speak to her GP about how she was feeling. Fortunately, she was happy to do this and I arranged to speak to the doctor about her. I arranged to see her the next day.

I spoke to the GP who was happy to see the lady and told me that she had had depression in the past. This had not been disclosed during her pregnancy and unfortunately, had not been readily available on the computer so I was unaware of this.

Visiting the couple the next day, I was pleased to see that the girl's mother was staying with the couple and had arranged to have the baby in her room the night before so that they could get some sleep.

The lady and her husband were feeling slightly better about things and realised that they couldn't look after their son without sleeping and eating.

We had a talk about how they could move forward. The lady had been offered medication to help her, but wanted to try and work it out for herself. I admired her for this but told her if she felt she needed some help she should be open to it.

I arranged to see her some days later and was surprised at how well she was doing. The baby was sleeping for six hours at night and feeding three hourly during the day. I was asked should I wake my baby during the night. My response to this was if somebody woke me in the night and gave me a plate of fish and chips, I would throw it at them. The baby knew when it needed feeding, they should go by that.

This lady did extremely well and was happy to be discharged on day ten. I told her she could always ring me if she was worried, but I knew she would be given a lot of help from our health visitors and would do well. And she did.

# How to Get Pregnant

A couple who came to one of my clinics were lovely but seemed very naïve. I asked about the pregnancy and I was told they were not yet pregnant but had come for some advice. I asked them to tell me how I could help them.

It turned out they had been married for 2 years but to put it bluntly, they had not got a clue how to get pregnant.

I had a long conversation with them and they told me they had both had very sheltered upbringings and really had not been told about the birds and the bees. They had both attended a boarding school run by nuns, but seemed to have had no sex education at either establishment. Well this was a first.

I had to ask them what they knew, and to my surprise it became clear they had not consummated their marriage. I fortunately knew the surgery had a leaflet that explained the birds and the bees and the basics of how to have sex and was worded really for young teenagers with the intent of educating them.

Showing the couple the leaflet, it became plain that this was new to them and they obviously needed time to digest the information. I knew from the conversation that they didn't have brothers or sisters and had been discouraged from using the internet.

I reassured them that the internet was safe to use and unsavoury things would not pop up every time they logged on.

My next suggestion was that they went home and read the leaflet and start practising. I actually felt very sorry for them. They fortunately were quite open to this, so we left it that they would contact me if they had any questions.

I had a couple of phone calls from them some weeks later and answered their questions to the best of my ability.

This couple came to seem me eight weeks later and she was pregnant. I was so pleased for them. I booked them for their pregnancy and was quite shocked when I was asked, well how and where does the baby come out? My answer to that was the same way as it goes in.

I arranged to go and see them at home so I could talk about pregnancy and birth with them. They obviously were quite concerned that they didn't know what was happening within her body.

This is the first and last time I have ever had to teach a patient how to get pregnant. The parents obviously hadn't informed them and apparently, they had both been to a same sex boarding school run by nuns so had not been given the tools they needed to know this. I have heard of sheltered upbringing but this is taking it to a new level.

This lovely couple did very well during the pregnancy. They attended all the ante natal classes and eventually had a normal delivery and a beautiful daughter.

They informed me that they would make sure that their daughter was taught about life in general as they feel they had both missed out due to their upbringing.

This is a very unusual situation these days, sometimes I think children know too much too soon. My grandsons have got to the age where they drop things in the conversation that I think whoops, should they know that yet? Its life I suppose, I would rather it was that way than for them to go through life without a clue of what's going on.

# Surrogate Parents

A couple came to my booking clinic and during the consultation, it was made known that the lady was carrying a baby for her brother. He was in a same sex relationship and they were so excited to be having a baby.

They were a lovely couple who had 2 children of their own and were happy to be carrying the baby for the couple. They made me laugh when I came to ask who the father was? It was either of the two new dads. Apparently, a turkey baster had been used and a mix of both the men's sperm so obviously it was not known which little tadpole could swim faster, their words not mine.

The booking was completed and I arranged for the lady to have a scan. I asked her if she had seen a solicitor about the ins and outs of surrogacy. It turned out they had and they had it in writing that the baby would be handed over to the true parents.

I got to meet the two dads during the pregnancy, they were lovely guys and so excited about having the baby. They asked me if they could all come to my ante natal classes and I told them I had no objection to them all coming. I was actually looking forward to it. I could see that they were going to make it fun and enjoyable.

This lady came to every appointment with either her husband or one of the new parents or indeed all of them. They told me that the lady was going to be the God Mother of the child and her husband was to be the God Father.

It came time for them to come to the Ante natal classes. Oh my goodness, they were hysterical. The fathers were just lovely and so into everything that was going on. They gelled with the rest of the group and bonded with all the other fathers. I heard later that all the fathers went out for a meal and apparently had a great time

During the classes, I was talking to them about birth partners and how many were allowed in the delivery room. I talked to them and asked them who they intended to have at the delivery. They told me they would all be there.

I gave them the labour ward matron's number and told them they should arrange either a phone call or a meeting with her as the rule was only two people at the birth. I was sure that if they made arrangements for all of them to be there, it would not be a problem. If there was any uncertainty, I told them to discuss having the baby at home.

It was decided between them at a later appointment that they had decided to have a home birth as the hospital was not too keen on so many people being at the birth. I just hoped I was around when they delivered. I also discussed with them the matter of the surrogacy and that the midwives who attended the birth could not get involved with the legal side of things, but would obviously provide the mother with her labour notes and the information needed to get the birth certificate.

The time came for this lady to deliver and I was so happy that I was able to attend. All the participants were in attendance and the atmosphere was very party like. The lady was very relaxed and coping really well with the birth.

They had decided that they wanted to have a pool birth so they were filling the pool when I arrived. They were singing whilst doing it. We whistled while we worked 'da da da da da da da'. They were so happy and so supportive to my lady, it was lovely to watch.

The labour was going well and the time came for her to get in the pool. Then the two dads appeared in the room with rubber gloves on, plus an apron and a very large sieve each plus a bonnet on their heads. I have never seen anything like it, they were an absolute hoot.

They had been to a shop and bought the biggest sieves they could find. They told me they were both on poo patrol and were intent on being very diligent in this.

The lady was doing really well so I told the family I was going to call the 2nd midwife, so that we could prepare for the birth.

The parents of the new baby asked me what I was writing? They seemed to think I was writing an essay on the birth. I told them I was just filling in the notes and that births incurred a lot of paperwork. This seemed to amuse them, so I informed them that after the birth, there was more forms to be filled in, the paperwork takes about an hour after the birth so they were very surprised at that. I told them that there was even more paperwork to do when I went back to the hospital as all the information had to be put on the computer as well.

The second midwife arrived and was amused at the antics of the new dads. I asked them who was going to cut the cord and they replied we both are. They told us they had bought a special pair of scissors to do this and they had them sterilised especially for the occasion.

The lady at this point announced that she felt the urge to push. We encouraged her to do what her body was telling her to do. I placed a mirror on the bottom of the pool so that we could see the baby emerging and make sure the baby's head came out slowly so that she would not tear.

The baby was born to cheering and tears, the parents were very excited and the lady and her husband were delighted in the way the birth had gone.

The two men then went out of the room and bought in their cord cutting scissors. They were enormous so that they could both hold them to cut the cord. This was done and the baby was handed to the parents.

This was a lovely moment, the men were so delighted with the new baby and looked so happy cuddling their baby boy.

The lady was got out of the pool and we delivered the afterbirth, then the lady wanted a shower. We took her to her bedroom and helped her into the shower. We asked her how she was feeling about the birth and the adoption and she was really happy with how it had all happened. She was happy that she would see the baby on a regular basis and said she would be a special auntie to him.

We settled the lady in her bed and went downstairs to the men and the baby. The baby was sleeping contently in her dad's arms. I asked them if they had got the baby's formula ready for the baby, so that they could feed him when he was hungry. They had decided between them that the baby would be breastfed for the first days until the milk came in and then the mother would express milk for the baby.

They would all stay at the house until this time and then go home which fortunately, was a short distance away. The couple had arranged to take paternity leave for the first two weeks of the baby's life and then as both of them worked from home, they would share the care between them.

This had been really well thought out and as I told them, it saved the midwife doing two visits, one to see mum and 1 to see baby.

We made sure mum was comfortable and baby was fine and then we left them to get to know one another. We left them with telephone numbers and told them that a midwife would visit or contact them, the same day probably in the afternoon as it was now 4 am.

This was an unusual situation but ended very well. The mother managed to cope with the baby leaving the house and continued to express milk for almost six months. The parents were wonderful parents and made a lovely sight taking their baby out for a walk. This situation turned out very well for all parties concerned.

# Difficult Patients

A family who were expecting their third baby had moved into my area. I met the lady at my booking clinic. I took her history and asked the usual questions about lifestyle and health. One of the questions we always ask is do you smoke or take any drugs? This lady answered no to both questions. I knew that she smoked as I could smell it on her but not knowing her well, I left it for the first appointment and decided to tackle that at her next visit. I did give her leaflets on smoking, drinking and drugs and told her if she had any problems, she could ring me.

I was visiting one of my ladies who lived opposite the lady above and whilst I was there, the Police knocked at her door, asking her about an incident that had happened during the previous night. My lady proceeded to tell me that at 1 am in the morning they had been woken by a lot of noise. The lady opposite, who was early on in her pregnancy had been in her garden in the nude fighting with another woman. Apparently, they were arguing about drugs. All I was thinking was no, I don't want to know this.

Obviously, I could not divulge that the lady was pregnant but I was obviously very concerned. I decided to speak to the GP and the health visitor to make a plan to support this lady.

The GP was aware of her past when she had taken drugs but the health visitor did not know, so we decided that we would keep a close eye on the family and I would offer to do her next visit at home, so I could hopefully assess the situation.

I visited this lady when she was 15 weeks pregnant but was unable to gain access. I left a note asking the lady to contact me but unfortunately, this did not happen.

A few days later, I drove past her house and saw that the door was open so decided to visit and ask if I could check her over. Fortunately, the lady was in and agreed to this.

It is quite difficult to bring up the subject of smoking, drugs and alcohol when you know the answers already. The lady allowed me to assess her and was quite open about having taken drugs in the past. I told her that I had heard from the grape vine that she had an altercation with a drug dealer, who apparently was asking for the money she owed.

I reassured her that I was there to help not condemn and if she asked for help with her situation, I could speak to the health visitor and come up with a plan to help her.

Thankfully, the lady was open to this suggestion so I phoned the health visitor from the house, so that I could make an appointment for us all to get together and try to help her. Fortunately, the health visitor was able to visit straight away and joined us to discuss a plan to move forward.

I phoned the drug dependency unit and they agreed to see her. I made an appointment for her and told her that I would see her the following week, but she could ring me if she was concerned about anything.

The GP was informed of what was going on and we told him that we had informed the lady that if she continued to take drugs, she was at risk of having her children removed from her care as she would not be fit to look after them.

This lady was true to her word and accepted the help that was offered and was managing to keep to her promise of not indulging in drug taking.

The rest of this lady's pregnancy was good and she attended her appointments staying drug free throughout.

She delivered her baby without any problems and brought her baby home, when she was two days old. I was pleased to see that she was drug free although, she was still smoking, but not in the house.

I discharged her on Day ten and didn't hear anything until about 3 months later, when I was informed that unfortunately she had begun smoking dope and taking drugs again. The children of course were deemed to be at risk, so they were removed from her care and put with relatives.

This is a very sad state of affairs, it is so sad to see a family torn apart but I hoped it would make the woman realise that she could not be a fit parent if she was high on drugs.

Shortly after this, I retired but I heard through the grapevine that the lady was pregnant again. Her children were still living with relatives but she was under the impression that she would be able to keep this child.

I heard later that she had delivered very early at 27 weeks of pregnancy and that the baby was in the special care baby unit at a specialised unit, and would be for some time.

This is a very sad situation; nobody wants to tear a family apart, but the health and well being of the children is paramount. I heard that the lady spent a lot of time with the baby but unfortunately, was denied the chance to take her baby home.

I heard later that she has since, had another baby who again was not in her care. I do wish this lady well and hope she manages to clean up her act.

# Birth After a Tummy Tuck

I had a lovely lady who was having her third baby, who had a tummy tuck years before. She was great. She was always cheerful and was what I like to call an earth mother. Nothing fazed her, her children were lovely and she always attended her appointments.

The difficulty came when she got to about 28 weeks pregnant. It was really difficult to ascertain which position the baby was in. Her tummy muscles were really tight and I must admit I found it hard to find the baby's position.

I never let on to this lady that I was finding it difficult and I was very fortunate that the baby was always in the right position and she delivered her baby with no problems.

My advice, have a tummy tuck after all your children not before. Make life easy for your poor midwife.

## BIRTH AFTER A BREAST AUGMENTATION.

I have had several ladies who have had breast implants. I had one lady who had surgery, who really wanted to breastfeed her baby.

It is always uncertain whether this would be possible, it depends on where the implant is put, either on top or below the muscle.

This lady did not know so it was a matter of wait and see. Her pregnancy went well and the time came for her to deliver.

She had a beautiful baby girl, 8 lbs and 4 oz and she had a normal birth so was discharged home on the day after the birth.

I arrived at her house and was invited in. Her baby was beautiful and was breastfeeding well. The lady's milk was not through properly on day two, but the baby looked well and was hydrated and nice and pink, so I was hopeful that she would have an adequate milk supply once it came in which is usually on day three.

I arranged to visit on Day five for the baby's blood test, but told them they could ring the office if they thought they needed a visit before then.

When I arrived in the office on the Friday, I was told that the lady had requested a visit the day before as she was worried about her milk supply.

A maternity health care assistant had visited and thought that she was doing well. The baby seemed well and was nice and pink so she had reassured her and arranged for me to visit the next day.

I arrived at the house and was pleased to see that the lady and the baby seemed to be doing well. She was sleeping for 3 hours in between feeds and seemed content. I talked to the parents about the baby's blood test and then said I would weigh the baby.

The blood test was performed and the baby bled well, this is a good sign that the baby is well, baby's that are not feeding well are difficult to bleed. I then went on to weigh the baby and was greatly pleased to see that she was almost back to her birth weight.

The lady told me that she had contacted her surgeon and had been told that the implant had been put under the breast muscle, so this is obviously the best place for the implants to go.

I had another lady who had the same operation, but had the implants put on top of the muscle. This lady was unable to feed and was quite disappointed. She was also worried about the press informing people about certain implants that could leak and cause problems.

I advised her to ring her surgeon and ask whether she had the offending implants in place. I heard later that unfortunately, she had the offending implants and would now have to make the decision whether they should be removed or not. I told her that this is not in my remit so was unable to advise her, but that she should speak to her GP and take their advice.

She told me that she had been advised to have them removed and replaced but unfortunately, she felt that she was unable to fund this venture at the moment. I would have hoped that if private hospitals had put the offending implants in, they should have replaced them. Unfortunately, this was not the case. The lady decided to wait and see what happened. I just hope that it turned out well for her.

# Ectopic Pregnancy

A lady came to my clinic for a booking appointment. I had met her in her previous pregnancies and I thought she looked very pale.

We started talking through her notes when she told me she had a lot of pain in her left lower abdomen and had some slight bleeding.

I asked her the usual questions: when did the pain start? how much bleeding have you had?

I decided that as she had the pain for two days, we should do something about it. I arranged for her to go to the early pregnancy ward at the hospital to have a scan, to ascertain exactly what was going on.

I gave her the notes she needed and asked her to ring me after her appointment to let me know how she got on?

Later that afternoon I received the call and was informed that she had an ectopic pregnancy on the side she had the pain. What was unusual was that she had a uterine pregnancy as well.

An ectopic pregnancy is a pregnancy that has developed in the fallopian tube and is not a viable pregnancy. The lady was prepared for theatre so that the pregnancy could be removed from the fallopian tube. This was done and fortunately the lady was able to continue with the uterine pregnancy.

Fortunately, the lady did well recovering from her operation and the pregnancy continued normally. Her only problem was that she had some pain over her scar as obviously, it stretched during her pregnancy.

This lady decided she wanted to deliver at home and I could see no reason why this could not happen. Unfortunately, her consultant did not agree.

I informed her that she could discuss this with her consultant at her next appointment. I told her that although she had complications with the ectopic at the start of her pregnancy, that was now resolved so I was happy for her to have a home birth. I told her that consultants were there to manage ladies who had complicated problems, fortunately her problems had been resolved and I would leave it up to her and her consultant to discuss the safest way for her to deliver and we would abide by that.

It was agreed that she could deliver at home and I arranged to go and visit her at 36 weeks.

I visited at the allotted time and was seeing this lady's house for the first time. Oh dear, it was a bit of a mess. I asked her where she wanted to deliver and then had the difficult task of telling her that she would need to clear an area so that it was safe for her and the midwives.

Fortunately, I was able to do this without upsetting the lady. This would be her fourth baby and apart from the cluttered house, I could not see a reason why she would not do very well in her delivery.

I was not around when this lady delivered but was informed by the midwives that the house was still an awful mess, but they managed to have a safe delivery and a beautiful baby boy. The lady and her family were happy with the outcome.

I visited this lady after she had her baby and as I had been told the house was an absolute tip. The parents and their children were happy, so there is not a lot I could do about the situation. The noise in the house from the children and the parents was ear splitting, the television was on, the children were playing noisy games on their computers and then the dog joined in. I must admit when I left the house my ears were ringing.

# Listening to Mum's Stories

My mum had five children. She told me a story about when she was expecting me. She went over her due date so was taken into hospital to have her labour induced.

There was a room of 12 ladies who were all in the same situation. When my dad arrived to visit her, a nurse brought a tray into the room containing 12 glasses of castor oil, which she gave out to each lady.

My mum took a sip and said as it was so disgusting she could not drink it, so she gave it to my dad and made him drink it. Hilarious.

My dad had gone to the hospital on his pedal bike, so he had a very uncomfortable ride home. He did make it home but only just.

When my dad visited the next day, the nurse was apparently perplexed that my mums labour had not started as all the other women had gone into labour. Mum was taken to the labour ward and was induced by having her waters ruptured.

Thankfully apart from a jippy tummy, my dad survived to tell the tale.

Taking castor oil is frowned upon these days. The purpose of the oil is to stimulate the lady's bowels, which in time will stimulate the uterus. The problem with this is it can also encourage the baby to have a bowel movement. This can mean the baby is in a polluted bag of waters and can send the baby into distress.

# Chickenpox

I remember when my youngest brother was born, my granny came to look after us. She was quite a stern lady who expected us to behave well.

On the second day she was there, she told me and my eldest sister off for lolling about. It turned out we had both got chickenpox which swiftly passed to the other sibling.

Mum came home some days later to a chickenpox outbreak. Fortunately, my baby brother did not catch it.

Some days later, mum and dad decided we should all go out for a walk. My eldest sister had just started her period so mum asked my brother who was about eight to go and get her a sanitary towel from the upstairs bathroom.

He did this but informed us that he had bought one for all of us. Bless him, he didn't catch on to why we were laughing.

We did eventually go out for a walk. We must have looked a mess, three children with very spotty faces.

# Another Home Birth

I was called out to a home birth at 1 am in the morning. When I arrived, I was met by a young couple who were having their first baby. They were very keen to have a low-key birth and had done a lot of research into how they could achieve this.

They were hoping to have a hypno-birth and had done classes on line to achieve this. They told me they had music that would help them achieve this.

The lady was doing well. She was calm and coping with her contractions very well. When I examined her I found she was already 6 cm dilated (she needed to get to 10 cm). I encouraged her to continue with what she was doing and we settled into a good routine.

I checked the baby and mum regularly and everything was going well. My only problem was the music. She had one tape that she had on a loop, so it was playing over and over again. By 4 am, I was ready to scream. The music was awful. Apparently, it was dolphins talking but just sounded like screeching, I would be so pleased when this lady delivered.

The time came to call the second midwife who I was very pleased to see. Fortunately for our nerves, she delivered very soon after this and the music came to a halt.

Once we had delivered the placenta and made sure all was well with mum and baby, we were able to leave.

The lady very kindly offered me a copy of her birthing music tape, which I politely declined saying maybe she could pass it on to a friend who was hoping to deliver in the same way. I just crossed my fingers that I would not be called out to the birth. I don't think I could have stood another seven hours listening to dolphins talking.

# Couple from Somalia

I was introduced at clinic to a couple from Somalia. They were lovely, they were very happy to be having their first baby. They told me they had arrived in England some years previously and were very settled and happy in their new home.

Their English was not brilliant but we managed very well to discuss her pregnancy and what needed to happen to help with the delivery.

I booked her for the hospital of her choice and made an appointment for her to have her first scan.

This lady was lovely. She attended all her appointments and was always cheerful and polite. I realised quite early on that they were living on the breadline. Her husband had a job in a warehouse and she was a housewife.

I arranged to visit this lady at home at 36 weeks so that I could make sure she knew what needed to happen to ensure she had a safe delivery and that she knew all the choices she had for labour and delivery.

On the appointed day, I arrived and was welcomed into the house by both parents. We talked about what she wanted from her birth and I asked what equipment she had and what she needed.

I was informed that she had some baby clothes but they were finding it difficult to buy the bigger things she needed like a cot, pram and car seat. I told her I would have a word with the health visitor and see if we could get her any help.

Olney is a fantastic place to live and there is a lot of ladies who are more well off, who are more than pleased to pass on equipment to ladies who were less fortunate.

I managed to get her to meet a lovely lady who had finished having babies who was more than happy to help her.

Before I could leave her that day, she insisted that I had a bar of chocolate which she had bought for me. I must admit I was reluctant to take it as I knew that they could have spent the money on themselves but I was reluctant to upset them by refusing. I did tell them that I was very grateful but that they must not think they had to give me anything. I arranged to see her at clinic two weeks later.

I saw this lady at clinic and she told me that she had been given a cot, a Moses basket, a pram, car seat and lots of baby clothes. I was so pleased for her. She also told me that the lady who had donated the equipment to her had been very kind and introduced her to other ladies, who lived near her and had indeed had a coffee morning in her house so that this could happen.

I had another family who moved into my area from the same place as this lady and she was wonderful helping them settle in and get to know the local people.

It's so nice when things turn out well. This lady went on to have a beautiful baby and continued to meet up with her new friends who had also had their babies. This was a lovely support group for all concerned and I quite often saw them all walking around the area with their babies. I wish all good things on them all.

# Who's the Dad

I booked a lady for pregnancy who was asking some fairly weird questions. I went through the questions on the notes with her and she asked me to leave the next of kin till the end of the consultation. Then the questions started. She told me she was not sure who the father of the baby was, it could be one of two. One was white Caucasian, one was Asian. I told her that her next of kin did not have to be the baby's father. It could be her parents.

Then she asked me how soon into the pregnancy she could find out the paternity of her baby. Unfortunately, I had to tell her that this could not be decided until after the baby was born. This was obviously not what she wanted to hear.

It was a really difficult position to be in. She was reluctant to tell her partner that the baby might not be his. I can understand this, but as I pointed out to her, her partner was white as was she, it would be apparent soon after the birth if the baby was Asian.

This lady had a lot to think about. I saw her frequently throughout her pregnancy and she was coping very well, she always had her partner with her so obviously, we did not discuss what she had disclosed to me.

I arranged by phone to visit this lady at home when she was 36 weeks pregnant, I told her that it was up to her whether her partner was home with her.

The day arrived and I was allowed into the house. The lady was on her own so it was a good time to catch up with how she was feeling.

The conversation was a bit weird, I asked her how she was feeling about what she had disclosed to me and she completely denied she had ever discussed this with me. I was informed that I must have mixed her up with another lady. This was obviously not the case but I went along with it as I did not want to put any pressure on her.

This lady delivered at 39 weeks, she had a normal delivery of a beautiful boy, and everything seemed to be fine.

I visited her at home and they were besotted with their baby, but the husband was asking why his baby had brown eyes when they both had blue. A difficult question to answer but I asked if any of his or her family had brown eyes and the answer was no. The partner told me that his grandparents came from Cyprus so maybe that was where the eye colour came from. I said well he was obviously special and if they had any other children maybe they would have the same colour eyes.

It was fairly obvious from examining the baby that he was Asian. He had what is called a Mongolian blue spot on his buttocks, which only Asian babies have. It was not up to me to disclose this to the parents. I just hoped that things would turn out well for the family.

I spoke to the health visitor and the GP about the situation but as they agreed, we could not discuss this with them if they didn't bring it up to us.

I discharged this lady on day ten and wished them well. The baby was gorgeous. He had thick brown curls and beautiful brown eyes. Fortunately, the lady told me that the whole family was in love with him so hopefully things turned out well for all of them.

I saw this lady a few months down the line and we had a chat, she told me that things were going well and nobody had queried the ethnicity of the baby so all was well.

Well, at least I had not lost my marbles and didn't dream up the scenario. I do hope that life carries on well for this couple and their baby.

# Eating for Two

A lovely lady and her husband came to my clinic for booking for their pregnancy. They were very excited and were into what she should eat, drink and do to help her have a healthy pregnancy.

I went through the pregnancy notes and discussed the care that she would receive. They wanted to deliver in our local unit and asked if they could see a consultant. As the lady was 42, I referred them to the Hospital Clinic and asked to see them again at 15 weeks.

The day arrived for the next appointment and the lady was doing well, her observations were all within normal limits and the baby's heartbeat was strong and regular. I asked if they had any questions and the husband asked if it was normal for the father of the baby to put on weight.

I answered with the comment. Anyone would put on weight if they eat too much. The husband then told me that since his wife got pregnant, he had been really hungry and had already put on 2 stone. His wife, who was obviously carrying the baby had only put on 7 lbs.

The lady told me that he had bought more new clothes than she had, as he had grown out of them. I told him that when the baby was born, she would lose the baby weight. He would not. I told him perhaps he should start a new clothes line for pregnant men.

We had a laugh about his eating habits and he confessed he was getting up in the night to scoff. His words not mine. I talked to them about eating a healthy diet and trying to cut out the sugary snacks. I was asked if I would weigh him and we did this and gave him a challenge. That he would not put on any more weight by their next appointment.

This lady's pregnancy went well and I saw them regularly throughout. The husband changed his eating habits and managed to lose the weight he had put on. He made me laugh about how he had put an alarm on the fridge so that when he opened it snorted like a pig.

The lady had a normal delivery and had a beautiful baby girl. She came home the day after the birth. The lady and her husband were delighted with their baby and did very well. She just had one problem.

The poor lady was very constipated and was obviously very uncomfortable. I got a prescription for her to try to solve the problem and thankfully, she managed to quite quickly resolve her problem.

I visited her the day after all this happened and the husband who was a bit of a joker told me he had something to show me.

I went into the garden with him and on a newspaper was the biggest poo I have ever seen. He told me he had measured it and it was 12 inches long and 3 inches wide!! No wonder she had felt a sense of relief after passing it.

He then went on to say she had sat on the toilet to perform but had stood up as she felt so uncomfortable, at that moment she performed and the poo landed on the floor which is why he had kept it to show me.

I did ask him what he was going to do with it and he told me if he tried to flush it down the loo it would block the system, so he was going to put it in his garden recycling bin.

We had a good laugh about it and I commented that I hoped the poor recycling men didn't see this contribution to their bin.

The lady was feeling much better and was obviously very relieved that her bowels were now back to normal. She told me she had stood on the scales that morning after the event and she had lost 5 lbs. I am not surprised, poor girl, she had really suffered.

# Breastfeeding

I booked a lady for her pregnancy and she brought her husband with her for the appointment. They were a lovely couple but were very intense and I noticed that the husband was writing down everything I told them.

When the appointment was almost over, I asked if they had any questions. The husband told me that he was going to be a stay-at-home father and was wanting to breastfeed the baby. I asked him what he meant by this and he told me that he had read on the internet that it was possible for a man to breastfeed a baby if he stimulated his breasts to produce milk.

Phew, that was a new one. I told him that I had heard about a contraption that consisted of a bottle, a tube and tape so that the man could simulate feeding, but I had never heard of a man who was able to breastfeed completely.

In my mind I had a picture of a baby on a hairy nipple. Not the best image to have but as the couple were so wanting this to happen, I told them that they should ask Dr Google about it, and I would speak to the GP to see what he thought! I arranged to see them some weeks later.

After my clinic, I spoke to a GP who was gobsmacked at the request and felt as I did that this would be impossible to achieve. The GP agreed with me that some men had man boobs and looked as if they might be able to feed but it was indeed ridiculous.

I saw this couple at their next appointment and asked whether they had any information for me about the situation.

The husband told me that in America, men who wished to breastfeed were given oestrogen to enable them to do this and that they had made an appointment to discuss this with the GP. I would have liked to have been a fly on the wall when this was discussed.

The lady's pregnancy proceeded normally and they were told that the GP felt unable to help them with their wishes. The husband had researched on the internet about oestrogen tablets and could buy them from an online pharmacist

I talked to them about buying drugs online, how dangerous it could be as some sites were not registered with a pharmacy that was recognised in this country and they really couldn't be sure what they were buying. I also told them that if the husband messed about with his hormones that this would not be good for him and could affect them if they wanted further babies. I told them they needed to think carefully before they proceeded with their plan.

We discussed the mother expressing her breast milk so that the father could feed the milk to the baby when she was at work. I told them that they could freeze the breast milk so that they had a supply for the time when she had to return to work.

The outcome to this story was that the lady had a normal delivery, she managed to breastfeed her baby and also to freeze milk so that she had a supply for when she returned to work.

Thank goodness for that, I had visions of this man starting a new trend for fathers.

I saw this couple when the baby was about three months old and the lady had already returned to work and the father was enjoying staying at home to look after the baby and the feeding was going well. He did tell me that he was disappointed that his plan had not worked but they were happy with things as they were.

Thank goodness for that, I don't think that there are many men who would want to breastfeed their babies, so I am happy that this was not the case.

# Injured Husband

I visited one of my ladies when she was pregnant as she had phoned me in a distressed state. I arrived and was allowed in and the lady proceeded to tell me that she was very worried about her husband who had been involved in an accident whilst at work.

She went on to tell me that he was in hospital after being involved in an accident on the M1 whilst at work. I asked her what had happened and she proceeded to tell me that her husband had been travelling in the back of an open back lorry and when the driver had stopped abruptly, he had fallen off the back of it.

I must admit I have heard of things falling off the back of a lorry but this was a first. I had to stop myself from laughing.

It turned out that her husband had been lucky, he could have been killed but had luckily just broken his leg. Obviously, this was awful but it could have been a lot worse.

Her husband was due out of the hospital that day so fortunately, he was not too badly hurt.

I knew that her husband was the only driver in the house so this could be a problem for the family, but I told her that as she lived in a village, I would do her ante natal visits at home until she could get to the surgery.

This lady was 37 weeks pregnant at the time of the accident, so it was not a good time to happen for them.

We discussed what to do when she went into labour and as her mother lived nearby it was decided that she would take her and her husband to the delivery suite. If the mother was at work, they would have to phone for an ambulance if they could not get anyone else to take them.

This lady went into labour two weeks later and fortunately, the mother was able to go with them and also able to bring them home.

The lady had an emergency caesarean section so was a bit incapacitated for a while. The family rallied around them and helped out when and where they could.

I visited this lady regularly and she did very well. I arrived on day ten to discharge her to find there was no one at home. I left a note asking them to ring me.

I heard back later that day from the lady telling me she had gone to register the baby's birth. She had gone on the bus, so it was a real journey for her. She told me she had taken two buses and it had taken her an hour to get to the office.

I was really upset that this had been so difficult for her and her husband. She had the baby, a pushchair and a disabled husband to get to the office.

I had been campaigning to keep the services of the Registry Office to continue to visit the local centres in Newport Pagnell and Olney but unfortunately, after several months, this had been stopped and now all parents needed to go to a central office in Milton Keynes. It was such a good service that they gave us and for a while they continued to come to the local offices, but unfortunately, it was stopped and this was why this poor lady had to go on such a trek? It's an awful shame but money talks and has to be saved somewhere. It's just a shame it had to axe this particular service.

# Mistaken Identity

*I was asked to go and help on the labour ward one evening as they were really busy. I arrived to find that a lot of baby's had been born but several ladies were waiting to come to the ward. I was asked to try and clear a room as quickly and sensitively as possible to allow this to happen.*

*I went into a room introduced myself and asked if the lady was ready for a shower and to be transferred to the postnatal ward. Fortunately, the couple were feeling up to doing this so I quickly got the lady in the shower, collected all her things together and when she was ready took her to the ward.*

*Arriving back on the ward I decided that I had better start cleaning the room as the ladies who usually did this were occupied in other rooms.*

*It was a very hot day and sometime later, I had cleared most of the room and was on my knees checking under the bed and lower surfaces that they were clean. I was aware that a lady had arrived at the door, dressed in scrubs and offering to help so I gave her a cloth and we quickly got the room ready for the next patient.*

*I did not have a clue who this lady was, apart from her first name but we seemed to be getting on like a house on fire.*

At that point the Head of Midwifery, came into the room and was talking to this lady, I quickly caught on that she was the new Head of Directorate.

I was gobsmacked, and when the Head of Midwifery left, I apologised to her for using her as a cleaner. She was lovely about it and laughed and told me it was a refreshing change to be treated normally and as one of the workers.

This lady was great, she stayed until the ward was calmer and all the ladies that had needed to come were with us.

Some days later, I was astonished to get a phone call from this lady asking if she could come out with me for a day and see how the community worked. Well, if she was up for it so was I.

The day arrived and I picked her up from the hospital and off we went. I discussed with her how she wanted me to introduce her to my ladies and we decided that she would be called by her Christian name and would like to be known as a midwife who needed updating. That was fine with me.

We had a good day. I was really busy and had several visits in fairly remote locations, so she was able to see how far I had to drive to reach my ladies and how much time this could take up.

In the afternoon we had my ante natal clinic and I had her checking blood pressures, testing urine and taking blood. She seemed to really enjoy herself and was very comfortable with the patients and their families.

I was pleasantly surprised that the Head of Directorate was happy to work as a midwife so that she could see how we worked and the difficulties that sometimes we had to overcome.

*At the end of the day, I took her back to the hospital and she told me she had enjoyed herself and wanted to continue to work as a midwife on a regular business. This is the first and last time I ever found that a senior manager was willing to work on the shop floor and I must admit I found it very refreshing.*

*We continued to work shifts together about once or twice a month until this lady who was a great manager had to reapply for her own job and unfortunately, was not fortunate enough to be able get the post.*

*I was sad to think that she was no longer working at the hospital. She was a great asset and a big loss. It seemed to be the usual thing with the NHS. If something works, change it. It sounds a bit cynical but I have seen this happen time and time again to the detriment of the service.*

# Who's the Father

*Soon after I started on community, I was asked by the GP to visit a girl at home to book her for her pregnancy. I was told that the family were well known to the surgery and lived in a small village nearby.*

*I arrived at the house, to be greeted by the parents and a girl of about 16 years of age. It was clear that the daughter had a few problems, such as not reaching her milestones. She was a rather large girl and apparently no one had realised she was pregnant, until the mother realised she had not had a period for several months.*

*The girl told me that she did not have a boyfriend and did not believe she was pregnant. Oh dear, this was a difficult situation. The mother was shouting at her that she must have had sex with a boy. The father just left the room.*

*The girl was pregnant and I booked her for the hospital of her choice. She was already about six months along and I let her hear the heartbeat so that she realised that she had got a baby inside her. I also arranged for her to have a scan so that we would have a better idea of the dates when the baby was due. I arranged to see her later after her scan.*

*I discussed this case with the GP and unfortunately, it was apparent that he thought the lady had become pregnant by someone inside the house. This is a very difficult situation, the girl had two brothers and also of course, a father, so it was unknown who the father was and we would probably never know.*

*The girl's pregnancy scan showed she was already about 27 weeks pregnant so more than half way through.*

*I got to know this family very well during this time and found they were dysfunctional, the language used if this house was horrendous, and I was shocked at times by the language of the youngest child who was five and had just started school. If my children had used the language he used, I would have been horrified, hopefully he would be taught at school that swearing was not appropriate. I could only imagine what the other parents would feel if their own child picked up some of his more-choice words.*

*The lady eventually delivered and had a baby girl. The delivery went well but it was fairly obvious the girl was struggling to look after her baby. Her mother stepped in to help and I think would have to do most of the care for this child.*

*I visited this girl and her family on several occasions and they were managing to cope with the baby needs between them. Unfortunately, the language had not improved.*

*Sometime later after I had discharged them, I was talking to the GP and he disclosed to me that he thought the girl's father had been the culprit, but with no evidence to prove this there was not much we could do about it. I just hope that if that was the case, then he would desist from continuing to abuse his daughter.*

*This is a shocking situation but very difficult to prove. The family continued to help look after the baby and much later on, I was this baby's midwife when she got pregnant.*

*The house was still messy and smelly and the language had not improved and the way they talked to one another left a lot to be desired, but they seemed to find all this normal so there was not a lot I could do about it but hope that this family found some way to get along peacefully.*

*This said lady went on to have two more children. She now had three children with three different fathers. One of her failings was she was always losing her notes. It takes a good hour to fill these in, so it was a real pain when this had to be repeated time and time again.*

*This lady made extra appointments throughout her pregnancy. I actually felt that when she was pregnant, was the only time she had any care and attention and I got quite fond of her, although she could test my patience at times.*

*She continued to see me as her midwife although, she had moved away from my area. I told her that I would not be able to visit her after she had her baby as she lived the other side of the city. I informed her that if she wanted to continue to see me, she would have to stay with her parents after the birth.*

*This lady had her baby and went to stay at her mother's house. Just before she delivered, her father had been taken ill and had unfortunately died. I was quite shocked when I visited that the girl openly told me that it was her father who had made her pregnant with her first child and her mother was aware of this. Her mother was in the room when she told me this and I waited for a comment from her, but nothing, then she commented, that's life it happens.*

*There is no answer to that, if she and her family thought that this was acceptable behaviour, it's really sad and unbelievable.*

# How I Changed My Ways

*I booked a lady for her pregnancy and was going through all the questions. I did my usual talk about what to expect and how she would be looked after and then began asking questions. We got to the medical history and to try and lighten the mood I asked have you got a wooden leg or a glass eye. To my horror, the answer was yes, I have a prosthetic leg.*

*I was shocked and apologised for saying it the way I had. Fortunately, the lady found it very amusing and told me she had been born with one leg that was missing below the knee and had Jimmy fitted before she was toddling. She called her leg Jimmy and it was a joke in their family. When she was very young, she would take Jimmy off and hide it and hop around the house telling her parents that Jimmy had gone missing.*

*She was a lovely lady and quite honestly you couldn't tell she had a false leg. The next chat we had was about blood tests and the flu vaccine that we offered to ladies. I was told she would have both but as she wasn't very fond of injections, she would prefer it if I gave her the vaccine in her false leg. We had a laugh about this but as I told her it wouldn't work as Jimmy was not amenable to this.*

*This lady had a worry that she would not be allowed a water birth because of her disability. I told her that we didn't* want her to swim the channel, just be comfortable in the pool and I saw no reason why she could not have such a birth.

I told her as she was very normal, she did not have to be referred to a consultant. This lady thought that because of her disability she would be treated differently to other ladies. As I told her she didn't give birth through her leg and the rest of her was normal. I arranged to see her after her scan and thankfully, she went away very happy.

I must admit after this lady's booking I never asked that question again. Someone else might not have taken it in the good humour as she did.

This lady had an uneventful pregnancy and did very well. She was concerned that as she put on weight it would put more stress on her leg but fortunately, this did not happen.

I was lucky enough to be in helping the labour ward when this lady was admitted to have her baby. I was concerned to find that she was quite tearful, she confided to me that she had been having dreams that her baby would be born with a short leg like her. I reassured her that she had several scans during her pregnancy and because of her disability this would have been carefully checked.

I have had lots of ladies who have had vivid dreams throughout their pregnancy. I can remember having them myself. It's very frightening for ladies but usually their dreams do not resemble the outcome at all.

This lady did really well in her labour and eventually was able to get in the pool. One of the midwives who worked on the labour ward and was in charge that night, was concerned that if we had a problem and needed to get her out of the pool this would be difficult due to her situation. I told the midwife *that I had promised this lady I would treat her as normal and was not going back on my word.*

*Her husband reassured the midwife and told her if there was a problem he would get in the pool and lift her out. Thankfully, the midwife was happy with this and left us to await the baby's birth.*

*This couple were so in tune with one another it was lovely to see. The lady was so relaxed and made my job really easy.*

*The time came when she had the urge to push. I told her to do what her body was telling her to do. She did this beautifully and before long, the baby's head was delivered quickly followed by a beautiful baby boy who was perfect.*

*The couple were delighted with their baby and the way they had delivered him. They cuddled their baby for a while and then I gave the baby to his dad whilst the mum was easily got out of the pool and dried and settled on the bed with her baby.*

*This lady had delivered a 9 lbs baby, she had no need for stitches and after the placenta was delivered, I left them to have family time whilst I made them tea and toast.*

*I was so happy for this couple who were really happy with their baby and were asking if they could go straight home. I did not see any reason why not and reassured her that I would get the paperwork done as soon as possible so that they could get home at a decent hour.*

*Once again, I was questioned about whether I should let this lady who had a disability go home so soon after the delivery.*

*I told the midwife that she had been born as she was and it was not hampering her looking after herself and her baby.*

*I carried on with the paperwork and when I went back into the room but was a trifle upset that the midwife had been into the couple and questioned whether they should be going home so soon.*

*I spoke to a doctor who thankfully agreed with me that there was no reason why this lady should not have an early discharge, so I quickly got the paperwork together, gave this to them and told them I would see them at home the next day.*

*Once I had put the room to rights and finished the paperwork needed, I could go home to my bed.*

*This lady coped really well with her situation and the baby breastfed well, he had put on a lot of weight and she was very happy when I discharged her on the tenth day.*

*This case shows that women should be treated normally and not how we think they need to be treated.*

# Out of Area

*One of my eldest daughters' friend was pregnant. She lived a few miles out of my area but was anxious to change her midwife who she felt did not understand her. I spoke to the GPs and arranged for her to come to my next clinic.*

*I met this lady at my next clinic, she was lovely but really anxious. I talked to her about her pregnancy and where she was having her baby and she decided that she wanted to change her mind and go to the hospital that I was attached to.*

*This was all arranged and the lady went away very happy. I got to know her very well. She was very sweet but suffered a lot of anxiety throughout her pregnancy. I reassured her that all was well but I found she was always quite tearful at her appointments. I got to know that apparently her first midwife had frightened her at her booking appointment telling her that as she was quite short she would more than likely have a difficult delivery.*

*I beg to differ. Height cannot predispose to a difficult delivery and even mentioning this to her had freaked the poor girl out. Fortunately, she had a normal pregnancy and eventually went on to have a beautiful baby girl.*

*I was lucky enough to be able to visit this lady postnatally and was pleased to see that she had bonded beautifully with her baby and was coping extremely well with the baby's demands. Her delivery had gone well but she was quite sore as she had some stitches.*

*This lady did very well and I was able to discharge her on her tenth day to the care of the health visitor.*

*We were lucky enough in Olney to have some classes after birth that were held for first time mothers, which were a really good way of meeting people and being reassured that they were doing well. This lady was able to attend these classes even though she lived just outside the area. It's a really good way of making sure that all ladies were coping with the situation they were in. Usually after the classes, the ladies all went to one of the local coffee shops to continue getting to know one another.*

*It is a known fact that ladies who make friends during and after their pregnancy usually stay friends for life.*

# A Delicate Flower

*A lady came for a booking appointment with her husband and it became clear that she was a little pampered by him. We went through the notes and talked about where she would like to deliver. The lady told me she was a bit worried about the blood tests as she did not like needles, and that her husband had volunteered his blood instead of hers.*

*Well it doesn't work like that. His blood was no good to me. It needed to be her that had the tests. Unfortunately, this came as a shock to them and her husband was concerned because his wife had to go back to work after her appointment. I reassured them that there was no reason why she could not go back to work as I was only taking a small amount.*

*The next question was do you think my wife should have a sick note so that she can rest at home? I reassured them that pregnancy was a normal thing and it was not necessary to rest all the time. Eat a healthy diet, do some exercise and keep doing what you normally do. I did remark that if all pregnant ladies were off work because of pregnancy, this would make it very difficult for employers.*

*The husband was so anxious and asked me if I would give her a note for her to have the next week off work?*

*Unfortunately, I had to tell him that I couldn't do that as it was necessary for a GP to do the certificate and I was not sure that they would be willing to do that as his wife was pregnant but she was well. I did tell them that if she was ill, she could self-certificate herself for a week and then see the GP. I told him that if his wife was unwell and not coping with her pregnancy and felt that she needed to be off work, she should discuss this with the doctor.*

*I arranged to see them at 15 weeks of pregnancy.*

*I had several phone calls from the husband worrying about his wife. I came to think he had me of speed dial. Bless him, he was so anxious. I tried to tell him that if he continued to worry, he would make himself ill.*

*The 15-week appointment arrived and the lady was doing well. The husband told me that they had bought a blood pressure machine, also a Sonic aid, (to listen to the baby's heartbeat) and they were constantly checking the baby and her blood pressure.*

*I talked to them about this and asked them what they would do if her blood pressure changed or they couldn't find the baby's heartbeat, as this was not always easy in early pregnancy. I was told that they had already been to the hospital twice as they could not locate the heartbeat.*

*I told them they would drive themselves mad if they carried on like this and would have to take up permanent residence in the hospital. I asked them what they thought would happen if all pregnant ladies worried as they did, the hospital would be inundated 24hrs a day with anxious parents.*

*The baby's heartbeat was fine and I arranged to see them after their 20-week scan. I told them they should try and relax and enjoy the pregnancy. I arranged for them to see the health visitor and also informed them about ante natal classes. I hoped that if they met other parents, they would relax and start to go with the flow.*

*I saw them several times before the ante natal classes started and they always had lots of questions and anxieties to overcome. It is awful when you can't reassure patients. They were still checking her blood pressure and the baby's heartbeat on a regular basis and were regular users of Doctor Google. I told them the NHS website was the one to use as a lot of wrong information can be given on some sites.*

*The ante natal classes were starting and I was hoping that this couple would learn to go with the flow. It was evident early on in the first class that they had done a lot of research about how to look after their baby.*

*I tried to tell the class that babies don't read books and they don't know what they should be doing. They cry when they are hungry or tired or just want a cuddle. Parents learn very quickly their baby's needs and become comfortable with them.*

*I always worry when people write down everything I said, but this couple went further; they recorded everything that was said. They also told me they were going to private ante natal classes. These were run by women who were not midwives but women who had babies and thought they could provide information for expectant parents. I told them it was up to them whose classes they went to but only NHS classes could provide the information about the different hospitals, and the choices they could make.*

*At one of the classes, we talked about birth, choices about pain relief and what they could do to help themselves. This* couple told me that they had been advised at the private classes that they should not have pain relief and should be plain about what they wanted and stick to their guns re their choices.

I always tell parents that they should be flexible with their wants and not to be too specific. All the parents in the class were having their first baby, so did not know how their labour would progress and how they would cope with the pain.

I was asked by this couple if I would look at their birth plan. I told them to bring it to their next appointment and we would go through it. I have seen birth plans before that are not achievable, they don't want pain relief, don't want interventions and wanted everything to be normal.

Believe it or not, all the midwives want is women to have a normal birth with no problems. Unfortunately, this does not always happen. Sometimes midwives have to call in the doctors to help babies come into the world.

I saw this couple at their next appointment and their birth plan was three A5 pages long. I told them that we would do the ladies check first and then discuss the plan.

It was fortunate that this couple had made their appointment the last of the clinic, as I knew it would take some time to read the birth plan.

The ladies check was good, everything was within normal limits and then came the plan.

The first thing on the plan was for the lady to be started off at 40 weeks as they did not want to go overdue.

It is much better for ladies to go into labour on their own as starting a labour off can take time and can be more painful.

The next request was that they should have no interventions at all.

I discussed this with them and told them that no one would make any intervention without discussing this with them, but did they realise that starting a labour off was an intervention. This came as news to them so I told them that hopefully they would go into labour on their own and would not need to be started off.

Then the views on pain relief. They decided that they wanted to have an epidural and wanted this given as soon as she went into the hospital.

I discussed with them that epidurals would not be given until the labour was established as this could slow things down and make it more likely that the labour would run into problems ending with either a ventouse, forceps delivery or a caesarean section.

The husband wanted to stay with his wife at all times. I told them that this was possible and the only way they would be parted would be if the lady had to go to theatre and needed pain relief before a procedure, this would only be for a short time and then the husband would be brought into theatre to be with her. He could also stay overnight on the postnatal ward with her and help look after the baby and her.

The next section of the birth plan was a bit more difficult to explain. The husband was against any other person, midwife or doctor examining his wife internally. He wished to be taught how to do this. I told them that this was a really difficult skill to learn and it would be impossible for him to be taught this as he obviously could not learn from other ladies who were in labour. He told me he wasn't silly and thought it would be easy to learn this art. I informed him that when a student midwife or doctor learns this skill, it is like going into the black hole of nowhere and feeling around to find the cervix and the dilatation. This did not go down very well and he told me he wanted to talk to someone in the labour ward who could facilitate this. I added that any midwife or doctor would not act on a husband's say so of his wife's dilatation.

I referred him to the labour ward matron who I knew would give him short shrift and tell him in no uncertain terms that this could not be done. I just wish I could have been a fly on the wall when this conversation took place. I cannot possibly write in this book what the matron said when I told her about this request, I was hoping she would ask me to be in attendance when this took place but to my disappointment she did not.

His next request was that they should have the same midwife throughout the labour. I informed them that they would have one to one care in labour, but shifts do change and any new member of staff that was to look after them would be introduced to them and brought up to date with the situation they were in.

The next thing was they wished to have a known person to deliver them, i.e. could I do it? I told them that I worked mainly on community and although delivered babies in the hospital, it would more than likely not be me as I had my clinics and other patients to deal with (I was praying at this point that I would not be available when this delivery happened).

The outcome of this case was that the lady went into labour at 37 weeks of pregnancy, when she arrived on the labour ward, she was already 8 cm dilated. They had actually allowed a midwife to check her cervix. She was too late for an epidural and apparently coped beautifully with the gas and air. Her husband apparently was like a scalded chicken, jumping up and down and panic stricken, he took more time to calm down than the lady took to deliver. A beautiful baby was delivered an hour after arriving at the hospital and she and her baby did very well. I cannot say the same about the husband, he was a nervous wreck.

I visited them at home some days later and he told me that the labour was awful and he could not possibly go through that again. His wife was a star and just replied, thank God women have babies and not men. I say amen to that. Bless him, he was still on edge making sure his wife and baby were fine and told me he was sitting up at night so his wife could get some sleep and then waking her, when the baby needed a feed.

I informed him that he would not be able to keep this up for long as at some point, he had to return to work and could not function without any sleep. He would be a danger to himself and any other person he came in contact with. This husband drove for a living so needed to be rested and relaxed.

I discharged them on day ten. Thankfully, by this time they were into a good routine and both of them were getting some sleep. The lady did beautifully and fortunately, her husband calmed down with time and realised that neither she nor the baby would break if he left them alone for a while.

I saw them several months down the line, when they told me that life was good, the baby was doing really well and he was realising that his wife could cope with the changes in their lives without falling apart. I wished them well, pleased that they were enjoying their baby and coping with the stresses that come along with this.

# Falling Out of Favour
# with a Consultant

I had a lady who lived in a village who had got to 38 weeks of pregnancy with no problem at all, but when I examined her abdomen, the baby was nowhere near her pelvis. The baby's head was in her abdomen. I talked to her about seeing her the following week and if the baby was still high, I would refer her to a consultant, who would decide the best way for her to deliver. I discussed with her that she may have to be delivered by caesarean section if the baby remained in this position.

This lady was lovely, she was quite happy for me to do this so that when I saw her the next week, I rang the hospital for an appointment as this baby was not anywhere near the pelvis. The lady was sent for a pelvic scan which is quite old fashioned and is not done these days, but this showed the outlet to her pelvis was very small.

I heard from this lady that she had been admitted to the hospital to be induced at 40 weeks. I told her I would see her on the ward the next day.

The next morning, I went to see the lady on the ante natal ward to find that the consultant had arranged for her to be started off that morning. I said I was pleased the baby was now in the pelvis, but was informed that it wasn't and they thought the consultant said that she should have her waters broken in the hope that the baby went into the right position.

Oh flip, this was not what I wanted to hear, I asked the lady if I could feel her baby and assess where the head actually was. This was agreed and the baby was still in the same position. I excused myself and went to talk to the midwife in charge of the ward. I explained my misgivings and she agreed with me that this was unusual with a first-time mother, but said that if that is what the consultant wanted to happen then it would.

I had grave misgivings about this as I thought inducing the baby with the head well out of the pelvis and with a small outlet could be impossible, and dangerous. The head needs to be pressing on the cervix to encourage it to dilate and this was not going to happen with this lady, unless the baby engaged into the pelvis.

I went down to the delivery suite to discuss this with the consultant, who frankly told me she was in charge of the lady not me and this lady needed to be delivered as the baby was large and the lady was not.

I still had grave misgivings and thankfully was able to discuss these with another consultant who was very approachable and I had great faith in his work. He told me he was on call for the labour ward from 9 am so that he would see this lady and assess the situation. I must admit I was very relieved, but a trifle anxious about what the other consultant would say.

I went back to the lady and her husband and told them what had happened, and asked them to let me know how things went as I was off the next day.

Later that morning, I had a phone call from the husband who told me that they had been seen on the labour ward and the other consultant was very reluctant to induce them as the head was very high. They had been advised to have the baby delivered by caesarean section so that it was safe for both of them.

I must admit I was very relieved to hear this as I could envisage this lady having a problem delivering this baby. I told them I would see them on the Friday.

When I turned my phone on the Friday, I had a message from the first consultant. Oh my goodness, she was ranting on about me interfering in her plans and who did I think I was? Flip, that was a bit difficult to hear but totally understandable.

I went to see the lady on the ward and she had a beautiful baby who for her was quite a good size, but totally gorgeous.

The delivery had gone well and the consultant had delivered her himself, he also told her that she would not have delivered vaginally as her pelvis was tiny. Phew, I must admit I was relieved that all was well and the parents were very happy with the way things had gone.

My next job was to go to the labour ward and have a conversation with the consultant who had left the message.

I was surprised to find that she was very nice about it all and told me that although she was very cross with the way I had spoken to her colleague, realised that in the end I was right. I told her I was sorry to have upset her but I was just concerned for my lady, I just didn't want anything bad to happen.

After this conversation, we left the best of friends and I must admit I admired her for the way she acted. I never ever had another problem with her and I greatly admired her and her work.

This lady did very well postnatally and thankfully was very happy with the way the delivery had gone. I never let on to her about my interaction with the consultant, it wasn't necessary for her to know and get upset, I was just happy that she and her baby were well and happy. I discharged her on day ten and all was well.

# A Troubled Marriage

Many years ago, I had a lady who was married to a policeman. Her pregnancy appeared to be going well and her husband always tried to come to clinic with her.

When she was about seven months pregnant, she attended clinic alone. She was very tearful and went on to tell me that her husband had left her. I was quite shocked, I must admit as they seemed such a lovely couple, but nobody knows what goes on behind closed doors. I talked to her about the situation, asking if she had a friend or family member who could come and support her for a short time.

It's always difficult when this type of thing happens, sometimes partners take fright at the enormity of becoming a father, I have seen this happen quite a few times.

All was well with the lady's pregnancy so I arranged to see her two weeks later, telling her she could ring me if she needed any more support.

I had a phone call the following week from the lady informing me that the police force had talked to her husband and told him he should come home and support his wife. I must admit I was quite taken aback by this. I had never known an employer getting involved in marital problems and wondered if this was the right thing for this couple.

The lady seemed happy with this and told me she was relieved that her husband would be returning home and asked me if I minded him coming to appointments with her. I obviously reassured her that this was fine and I wished her well, telling her I would see her the next week.

This lady's pregnancy went well, but it was obvious that there was tension between the couple. It was a difficult situation for both of them.

The outcome of this situation was the lady delivered just after her due date, she and her baby did well and husband supported her until the baby was only two weeks old, then he left again and this time he stayed away. Thankfully, he supported her and their baby financially.

It is obviously not a good idea to try and interfere in patients' marriages, only the couple involved know what is going on in their lives and have to sort it out themselves. This lady moved away from my area to live near her parents, who could support her with her baby. I hope things turned out well for her and her baby.

# Why Do People Interfere

I have had so many women ask me questions at clinic about a comment someone has said to them. I will give you some examples.

Someone at work thinks my baby is small. My reply, is this person a doctor or a midwife? the reply is usually no. Well, why take any notice of them? Let's check you over. Usually the growth of the baby is fine. I tell the lady to tell anyone who makes comments that her baby is growing beautifully and your midwife thinks it's perfect.

The lady in Tesco thinks I look too big. Oh flip, it's so difficult to tell women that people are always making comments to pregnant ladies. I remember when I was pregnant, some lady coming up to me and touching my bump saying oh, I love pregnant women. My instinct was to say get off leave me alone but being polite, I just smiled and moved on.

I was with my daughter Emma when Edward and George were a few months old, oh are they twins? yes was the reply. Are they identical? yes, they are. The next question was mind boggling, is it one of each? Ugh no, they are identical. Well, it can still be one of each can't it?

Another gem is, oh you cannot be seven months pregnant, you look ready to deliver, I think you should question your due date. I tried to reassure ladies but it happened over and over again.

Obviously, women who are pregnant are vulnerable, they don't always believe what random people say to them, but it does put a seed of doubt in their minds.

My advice, listen to your doctor of midwife, try not to be influenced by random members of the public who feel the need to comment on your pregnancy.

# Annoying Call Outs

New Year's Eve about 7 pm, I got a call to go to a baby that wasn't taking his feeds well. The mum had phoned the labour ward saying the baby would not settle and was crying during feeds. I drove to the house and was invited in.

The first thing that I was told was that the baby was very unsettled and they were due to go out to a party, so could I help them settle her? I asked the usual questions, how are you feeding? when did baby last feed? and is the baby filling his nappy regularly?

I was told the baby was bottle feeding. He had taken 3 oz of milk three hours earlier. The baby was only two days old so this was quite a large amount of milk to be taking at this early stage. I asked what milk they were using and was told they were feeding the baby with stage two milk, which is actually the follow-on milk for babies and is not suitable for new born babies.

I asked them if they had any first stage milk and was informed, they hadn't as their family had told them they would get more sleep if they used the follow-on milk. Oh flip, I told them that the baby was finding it difficult to digest his milk and it was too heavy for him. I asked the husband to go online and look for a chemist that was open so that they could buy suitable milk.

This did not go down very well and I was told they had not got time to do this so why didn't I just sort the baby out so they could go to their party.

I had observed the baby whilst I was talking to them and it was obvious, he was uncomfortable. I managed to get some wind out of him and he seemed to settle. I told them that if he fed 3 hrs earlier, he was due for another feed. I knew they would have problems if they continued to feed the follow-on milk, so I suggested the mother make up a feed with two scoops of powder to 3 oz of cooled boiled water so the milk was diluted, until they could obtain the milk required.

Diluting milk like this is not really what we should be doing but as no shops or chemists appeared to be open, there was not much else to be done.

The feed was made up and I gave it to the baby, who took around 2 oz and settled after winding. The parents asked me to give the baby the other ounce of the milk so that he would sleep whilst they were out. I advised them not to do this as the baby's stomach was not able take large amounts.

The next thing was the baby was put in the car seat and I was escorted to the door so that they could leave. I was a bit gob smacked I must admit, but told the parents I would talk to their midwife the next morning and make sure they had a visit to make sure all was well.

I drove home from this call a bit bemused by the parent's priorities, but not everyone is the same so I wrote it down to experience.

I had not been home long when I got another call to go to a couple, who had rung in and told the labour ward that the baby's cord was bleeding. When speaking to the labour ward leader, I was informed that the baby was five days old and they had no other problems. I told her that the baby's cord might leak at five days old but it couldn't bleed as it had dried off. Unfortunately, they had not taken a phone number for the couple so I made my way over to see them.

It took me nearly 30 mins to get to the house as it was at the far end of the area that we cover. When I got to the house, there were no lights on but I knocked on the door. After knocking several times, the husband leaned out of the bedroom window and told me I was not needed as the bleeding had stopped.

I told him as I was here I would like to see for myself, to set my mind at rest. I was really thinking you called me out so I wasn't going to leave without satisfying myself that all was well and they wouldn't call me out again that night.

The husband reluctantly let me in and I looked at the baby's cord area. The cord was actually off and the blood they were concerned about was no bigger than the end of a matchstick.

I told the parent's that some leakage was normal but as the cord was off this was nothing to worry about, so I bid them goodnight and left to once more drive home.

Believe it or not, I had not been home for 5 minutes when I was asked to go to a home birth. I made my way to the house and was invited in. The lady was having her first baby and was having contractions every 15 mins lasting 20 seconds.

I checked the lady over and all observations were normal. I asked if I could examine her and she agreed. This lady was not in labour any more than I was. Her cervix was not dilated at all and was not favourable (soft) for labour.

I stayed with them for an hour and told them that I would leave them to get to bed and get some rest for, when labour did start. They were amenable to this and I once again drove home.

When I reached home, it was 4 am so I felt I had had a wasted night and I was due on duty five hours later. I must admit I was a bit grumpy, when I got into the office the next day and fortunately, I was able to work until lunch time and then go home.

The lady who had thought she was in labour did not deliver for another two weeks and she called the community midwives out five times on false alarms, but in the end had a lovely home birth with no problems.

# Hair Loss in Pregnancy

A lot of ladies lose hair during pregnancy, but most don't. Some ladies say their hair is better whilst they are pregnant than before.

I remember one lady who, when she was 15 weeks pregnant lost all of her hair. It was obviously very distressing for her and we supported her as much as we could. She was provided with a wig by the hospital and thankfully as soon as she had her baby, her hair grew back very quickly. This lady went on to have two further pregnancies but never had the same problem.

My daughter Emma when she was pregnant with Edward and George lost an awful lot of her hair. She had beautiful long auburn hair which flowed to her waist and it was thought that it was because of this, it was making the problem worse. It didn't come out completely but was very thin and sparse.

I took her to my hairdresser who advised her to have her hair cut much shorter. Emma had twelve inches of hair cut off and it was so sad to see her in this state, but I kept reassuring her that it would grow back, when the boys were born.

Her hair did grow back but obviously, it took a long time to get to its former length. To this day she still has beautiful auburn long hair. I always tell her she is lucky and needs to thank her mother for this. I have auburn hair which although it has faded slightly, I have still not gone grey.

# Tall Lady, Small Baby

I had a gorgeous lady attend my clinic for a booking. She was six foot tall. Slim with lovely black glossy hair. I booked her for pregnancy and she decided she wanted to deliver in the hospital and go home soon after the birth if that was possible. Her husband was with her and was happy with this and backed her in all her requests. We talked about diet and healthy living and then discussed and took her bloods with her agreement. I booked her scan for her and asked to see her again at 15 weeks. They were supplied with phone numbers in case of any problems.

I saw this couple regularly throughout their pregnancy. All appeared to be going well until at 28 weeks when I thought that the baby was small for dates. I measured her abdomen and thought that she was measuring 25 weeks, so discussed with them about going for a scan to make sure the baby's growth was correct for gestation (weeks of pregnancy). They agreed to this and I arranged to see them again three weeks later or sooner if they were worried.

I had a phone call from this lady telling me that the scan showed that her baby's growth was on par with her stage of pregnancy, so I agreed to see her two weeks later. I was pleased about this and told the lady that because she was tall, she was obviously hiding her pregnancy well.

This lady was seen regularly throughout the next six weeks and each time, I thought her baby was small for her dates. When she got to 34 weeks, I measured her abdomen at 31 weeks. I discussed this with her and she again agreed to go for a scan. This lady told me she would ring me after she had attended for her scan. I asked to see her two weeks later.

A phone call from the lady told me that the scan showed her baby was growing well and was appropriate size for her dates. I was beginning to think I was losing the plot. I told her I would see her the next week.

At my next clinic I had a colleague with me, who was new to the area. I spoke to her about this lady and agreed that I would get her to measure her abdomen and see what she thought.

The lady came to clinic and we both examined her. My colleague thought her size was on par with her dates but I still thought she was showing up small for her dates. I discussed this with her and asked her if she minded seeing a consultant to set my mind at rest. This was agreed and an appointment was made for her the following week.

The consultant saw this lady and agreed with the scan that the baby was growing well. I was happy with this, but I continued to have my doubts.

This lady went into labour a day before her due date and went on to have a beautiful baby girl who weighed 5 lbs 4 oz. The labour ward staff asked her if anyone had queried the growth of the baby.

Fortunately, the baby was well and fed beautifully so was discharged home after two days. I visited them at home and was really pleased the baby was doing so well, but a bit shocked that the scans had showed normal growth. The lady told me that me that the afterbirth had been small and had been gritty. (This shows that the afterbirth was not feeding the baby well).

The lady and her husband were shocked that their baby had been so small, but as I told them the baby was fine piling on the weight and had no ill effects. I was silently pleased that I hadn't lost the plot, and could still be let loose on the pregnant ladies in the area.

# Big Dogs

A lady had delivered in a village near where I lived, so I was asked to visit her. I had not met her before but knew it was her first baby. I arrived at the house and when I knocked on the door, I heard dogs barking. The door opened and I was invited in.

They had two dogs, Irish Wolf Hounds. They were enormous but very friendly. I introduced myself and we all went into the lounge where the baby was sleeping.

I was talking to the couple and was amused to find I had both dogs sitting in front of me and looking at me. I stroked them as I was talking and the next thing I knew, they were both sitting on my lap. I could barely see around them. The couple were amused and told me I was honoured as they didn't sit on everyone's lap. Well, that was all very well but I couldn't move. I asked if I could wash my hands before having a look at the baby, and this was agreed.

I managed to remove the dogs and lift the baby from his crib. I examined the baby and found all was well. He was a lovely colour and feeding well. I placed him back in his cot and sat down again to continue to talk to the parents.

The same thing happened. The dogs came back onto my lap. It is very difficult to write notes with two huge dogs in front of you. They were very interested in all that was going on and were reluctant to move. It was very funny and we were all laughing. I asked the couple how the dogs were with the baby, and was told they were fine. When the baby cried, they howled to make sure that they picked the baby up quickly.

They went on to tell me that they didn't leave the baby in the room with the dogs if either one of them were not there. I said that was a good idea as though the dogs were friendly, no one knows how they would react if left alone with them.

I left the family to it and arranged for them to be seen the next day for the baby to be weighed. I was asked to send someone who liked dogs. I told them that when I rang the office in the morning I would pass on their message, but they may have to put the dogs away. I left the house and when I got back to my car, I was covered in dog hairs.

# Strange Places to See Patients

Many years ago, there was a rule that said if a patient lived inside our boundaries but had a different doctor, should be visited and looked after by us. My ladies who lived over the border should be seen by their midwives.

I fortunately had not got many ladies living over the border, but I had picked up several that lived in our area so we needed to look after them.

I contacted these ladies and made arrangements to see them at their homes.

One of the first ladies I saw, was lovely and seemed surprised that I wanted to see her at her home address. I told her she could come to my clinic if she preferred but she was happy for me to visit her at home.

A date and time was arranged and I was invited into the home. We talked about her pregnancy and I asked her what blood tests she had had? I was informed that she hadn't had any blood tests as the midwife had felt unable to do them. I was a little shocked by this but was informed that the booking appointment, which is where we first meet the lady and fill in her notes was performed in a park in the midwife's car.

I was absolutely shocked by this but was informed that the midwife always did this and it was well known with her patients. I did wonder if her managers knew this as it is highly unusual and not very professional.

I took the ladies blood with her permission and arranged to see her at a later date.

Thinking this was a one off, I put it to the back of my mind but was surprised when I met several other ladies that this had also happened to them. I did speak to my manager about this but as the problem was now solved by me seeing them, I don't know whether anything was ever done about this. I tried to contact this midwife on several occasions but was never able to get through to her but fortunately, I had no problems with these ladies so it was not too important that I spoke to her.

Apparently in the warm weather, I was informed that this midwife sat on a park bench to talk to her patients. This I could see no problem with but I was sceptical that it was right to examine a patient on a park bench. The mind boggles. I know that this midwife had a surgery she was working from so found it difficult to understand why this was happening. Unfortunately, I never found out but would have loved a conversation with her.

This arrangement did not last very long as new management changed it back to how it was originally, so I never did find out why it was happening.

# Difficult Times for a Patient

I booked a lady for her second pregnancy. This lady had unfortunately had a stillbirth with her first baby so of course, she was very anxious. I went through the notes with her and arranged for her to have an early scan and an appointment to see the consultant.

Unfortunately, no reason had been found for her first baby dying and this makes it very hard to reassure a lady when this is the case. I told her she could see me as often as she needed to as I wanted her to have the reassurance, she needed to enjoy her pregnancy. I took her bloods and arranged to see her when she was 15 weeks pregnant. I reassured her she could ring me at any time.

I saw this lady very regularly throughout her pregnancy and although she was anxious, she had a lot of support from her husband and family so felt she was coping well.

It was arranged for this lady to have a caesarean section at 38 weeks as her last baby had unfortunately died when she was 39 weeks pregnant. She was happy with this and was looking forward to the birth and obviously taking her baby home.

This lady came to my clinic three days before her baby was to be born and was obviously stressed, I tried to reassure her and told her if she was worried in the following few days, she could ring me or go to the hospital. This was important as I hated the thought of her getting herself upset before her baby was born.

I arranged to see this lady on the ward the day of the delivery to give her some support.

The day arrived and I went onto the ward to see her and her husband. She was really anxious but I listened in to the baby's heartbeat for her so that she was reassured. I also told her she was first on the list so wouldn't have to wait too long. We had a hug and I asked the husband to let me know when the baby arrived, obviously after he had rung family.

I received the phone call about two hours later. A beautiful baby girl had been delivered who was very healthy. This was really good news and after congratulating them, I told them I would see them the next day to have a cuddle. Fortunately the hospital I was assigned to, let husbands stay on the ward with their partners so they could help with the baby.

This lady and her baby did very well and were discharged home a few days later. I saw them at home and all was well with baby, mum was struggling with the lack of sleep and baby being upset during the night. This is obviously a normal anxiety for new mums and I tried to reassure her about this.

It's always difficult for mums who have lost babies to realise that this baby is normal and nothing is going to happen to this baby. I often find these mums are really hard on themselves and want everything to be perfect. This can be really difficult for them and they need time and support to get through this. I arranged to see her the next day and left her with phone numbers, in case she had any problems.

On the visit the next day, I found a very upset lady, her baby had a sore bottom and she was so upset about it. I reassured her that this was normal and lots of babies had this problem. Unfortunately, this lady wanted everything to be perfect and didn't want anything to be amiss with her baby. We had a chat about this and I told her that she was very normal, all new mums wanted everything to be good with their baby but babies don't read books, they don't know what they are supposed to do. I did manage to get a smile out of mum but it was so difficult for her. I was off until the weekend, but I arranged for a support worker to visit her in the meantime.

I was quite worried about this lady, so I spoke to her GP and discussed what was happening with her. He was fantastic and told me he would go and visit her and congratulate her on the birth and see if she opened up to him. I also spoke to her health visitor so that she was aware of what was going on.

This poor lady really struggled with life for the first few weeks, I visited her regularly and kept on reassuring her that she was doing well and the baby was thriving. She confided in me that she wondered if she was good enough to be a mother. That is really sad and I hugged her and told her she was doing great. I also encouraged her to go to the first-time mum's class so that she could meet other new mums, who were going through the same feelings and concerns that she was.

It took her a good six weeks to start enjoying her baby and to stop worrying so much. She had gone to the classes and met other mums who had been very supportive to each other. The only thing was she was now feeling guilty for the way she had reacted to the birth and the first few weeks of her baby's life.

I told her she was a normal mum who had unfortunately, had a difficult start because of what had happened to her with her first pregnancy.

It is so difficult to support these women who have had a loss, they are so anxious which is obviously normal and need a lot of tender loving care.

# Another Home Birth

I was used to the phone ringing in the middle of the night, so was not surprised when this happened at 1 am on a Sunday morning. I spoke to the delivery suite coordinator and was asked to make my way to a lady, who was having her first baby who lived over the other side of our area. I made my way to the house and was invited in.

The lady was having contractions regularly every five minutes and seemed to be coping very well. I asked the normal questions and then took the normal readings of temperature, pulse blood pressure and proceeded to palpate her abdomen for how the baby was laying and then listened into the baby's heartbeat. I was a bit hesitant about the way the baby was laying, I thought the baby could be breech but was a little uncertain as the lady had very good abdominal muscles, so it was difficult to ascertain. All was normal with the other readings and when I examined her, I found she was already 6 cm dilated, the presenting part was very high so if was difficult to ascertain what was presenting, the head or the bottom. I told them what I thought but they told me they knew the baby was head down so they were not worried. Well, that's alright then!

I told them that if the baby were to be breech, this was not something that should happen at home and they should think of relocating to the hospital. This was met with a big no. They would deliver at home and all would be well. I hoped they were right, but I did have reservations.

Whilst I was looking through the pregnancy notes, I asked them about any scans that they had and was informed they had not had any scans during the pregnancy.

We discussed what she wanted to achieve through her labour and delivery and had she any wishes that she wanted me to take into account.

Oh flip, that's when the requests started. They didn't want any interference with the labour. They wanted to get on with it without any checks from anyone. I suppose I should be grateful that I had been allowed to examine her.

They also requested that they should be allowed to deliver in the bedroom whilst I stayed in the lounge.

They did not want any pain relief or any injections for the afterbirth. Also, they did not want the baby to have Vitamin K after the birth (this is an injection that helps the babies blood to clot, some babies don't do this well but we don't know which ones, so all babies are offered this).

I was also told that I should feel pleased that they had rung me as they had thought about delivering on their own with no midwife present. Oh God, why do I always get them? I asked if they had discussed this with their own midwife but was told they had not, as they thought they would be refused a home delivery. They could be right.

I talked with them and told them that as a midwife I was happy to be hands off but felt very uncomfortable about being in a different room when they delivered as if anything were to go wrong, this would probably lose me my registration.

It was discussed that they should have a talk between themselves to discuss this and I would ring the delivery suite to discuss this with the midwife in charge. This was agreed and they went off into the bedroom to chat.

A phone called was made to the senior midwife who was a bit gob smacked and agreed with me that this was fairly ridiculous and should have been sorted out before the lady went into labour. I told her that I thought the baby was breech and that the lady had no scans during the pregnancy. She groaned at this and agreed with me that the supervisor of midwives should be informed, so that she was aware of what was going on. I also asked that the second midwife should be called so that I had some back up in case things got difficult. This was agreed and it was agreed that the supervisor would ring me when she had been contacted. As a supervisor myself, I knew that there was not a lot that they could do but support us and they needed to be informed in case any problems arose later on.

The couple eventually came out of the bedroom and told me that I could stay for the delivery but only on their terms. I should not listen in to the heartbeat unless they asked, I could be in the same room for the delivery but be standing back and not interfere in any way unless asked.

Oh my goodness, why do people act like this? we are there to help and make sure that the lady and her baby are well with no problems to either of them.

They informed me that they did not want the baby to have a cord clamped after birth, but wanted to use cord ties instead. By this time, I was thinking it was time for me to retire, as the woman's requests were getting more bizarre and I was finding them more difficult to deal with. I wondered in my own mind, why women put themselves at risk like this?

It became clear that this lady's labour was progressing quite quickly so when the doorbell rang and the second midwife appeared, I was very pleased to see her. I quickly got her up to speed with what was happening and the requests the parents were making. This was met with groans and for a minute, the air was a bit blue. I told the midwife we could only do our best to make sure we documented everything as it happened and be ready to step in when the time came for the delivery. I also asked the second midwife to be aware that if things started to get difficult with the delivery that we should think of calling an ambulance.

The lady soon showed signs that the delivery was fairly imminent. She was feeling pressure and was getting ready to deliver her baby. She decided she would deliver in the lounge, so we made an area ready to receive the baby.

Up to this point, I had only been allowed to listen in to the baby once so I kept asking the mum if the baby was still moving, this was usually ignored but was asked anyway.

I had told the other midwife that I was unsure about the baby's position and she informed me she had never delivered a breech baby, so was glad I was there. No pressure then.

Then the lady started to push and a bottom appeared, the husband started to panic and I told the lady she should sit on the edge of the settee and allow me to help her. Thankfully this was agreed, and I sat on the floor and did the manoeuvres for a breech birth. This lady actually did very well with no help from her husband, who was freaking out. Fortunately, the other midwife was trying to keep him calm whilst I delivered the baby. Thankfully, the baby was born with no problems but was quite slow to cry which increased the husband's stress.

Fortunately, after a bit of oxygen, the baby soon cried and all was well much to everyone's relief. The placenta was delivered with no problem, the cord was cut and tied as the parents requested. The lady did not need any stitches and the blood loss was minimal. I was very relieved that all was well but felt about twenty years older than when I arrived.

The baby was weighed and was 9 lbs 4 oz, so we felt fortunate that the baby had delivered with no problems. The delivery suite and the supervisor of midwives were informed of what had happened and were obviously pleased with the outcome.

The baby was being breastfed by the mum and the dad had calmed down and was apologising for the problems they had caused with their requests.

I must admit I was glad when the lady and her baby were tucked up in bed and we were able to leave to return to the hospital to refill the bags and complete the computer work. It was time for the day shift when we had finished so thankfully, we could go home to our beds.

I talked to this lady's midwife about what had happened and was informed that none of their plans had been discussed with her when she visited them to talk about the home birth. She was very apologetic but as I told her it wasn't her fault and all was well at the house, apart from our nerves being frazzled.

# Called into Help on the Delivery Suite

One evening I had a phone call, asking me to go in and help on the unit as they were extremely busy. I made my way in and was asked to go into a room and look after a lady who was having her first baby and was doing very well.

I went into the room and introduced myself, I asked about her pregnancy and any problems she had during pregnancy. She and her husband told me she had suffered a lot from nausea and vomiting in the first 16 weeks of pregnancy but apart from that it had been plain sailing. She had all the necessary blood tests and scans and all had been normal. I asked them if they had any requests for their labour and delivery.

They had made a birth plan, which I went through with them but really they told me they were open to anything that would ensure the safety of mum and the baby. This is the kind of birth plan I like, no demands, just go with the flow and any help they needed would be accepted.

All the readings of her blood pressure had been normal, the baby was laying a good position, its heartbeat was regular and the contractions were regular every three minutes. The lady was moving about the room and was coping beautifully with her contractions.

The lady was examined to determine her cervical dilatation and I found she was already 8 cm dilated. I encouraged her to keep moving and sat quietly writing my notes watching and waiting.

Fairly soon after this, the lady decided she would like to use the birthing pool so I left the room to enquire as to if there was a pool available. Fortunately, there was, so I started filling the pool and moved the couple into the other room. Soon after this, the lady got into the pool and found it very helpful with relaxing her during her contractions. The baby's heartbeat remained stable and it was clear that she was getting ready to deliver her baby.

Shortly after this, she felt the urge to push so I told her to do what her body was telling her to do. I encouraged her to relax between her contractions, to save her strength for pushing.

In no time at all, the baby's head was crowning and I asked the lady to pant like a dog so that the head delivered slowly to prevent her tearing. She looked at me as if I was potty and said, pant like a dog? yes, I said.

Then the fun started, with the next contraction I said pant and she woofed and woofed and woofed until the contraction was over. Her husband was laughing and I just said, well if it works for you carry on. The lady when the contraction was over could not understand why her husband was laughing. He just told her you make a lovely puppy.

For the entire time until the head was delivered, she woofed. It was great to watch, very amusing but really effective. Her husband decided to film her on his phone so that he could show her when it was over.

Once the head was delivered, we waited for the next contraction and the baby was brought up out of the water onto the lady's chest. She had done so well and was delighted with her baby. Shortly after this, the placenta was delivered and the cord was clamped and cut, and mum and baby were helped out of the pool onto the bed to have some skin-to-skin time.

It was at this point that the husband decided to show his wife the recording of her woofing. The lady laughed and said she hadn't realised she was woofing, she thought she was panting. I just told her she had done very well and whatever noise a woman makes is fine with me.

I cleared up the room, made the lady and her husband some tea and toast and left them to have some family time whilst I finished the notes. One of the midwives asked me what the noise was all about coming from the room? I explained to her about the panting or woofing and she said it sounded as if there was someone coughing constantly in the room. The other midwives found it amusing but as I said it had worked for her, so it was fine with me.

I was informed that my lady had been the eighth lady to deliver in two hours. By this time, all the rooms were full and there were no more labouring women so things were calming down.

Going back into my lady's room, the baby was breastfeeding and mum and dad were delighted with their child. Once the baby had finished feeding, I helped her into the shower and left dad to cuddle his son. They were both keen to go home that evening, so I made the lady comfortable and went out to finish the notes so that they were not hanging around for hours.

Sometime later, I was able to discharge my lady with her baby and once the room was cleared and cleaned, I was able to leave the labour ward. It had been a long night and I was able to go home to my bed. The labour ward at this time was now empty and was ready to receive ladies again. It is life on a delivery suite, sometimes it's so busy you wonder how you will get through it and at other times it's eerily quiet.

# Different Religions

One of the ladies attending with her husband I booked for another midwife disclosed to me that she was a Jehovah's Witness. I talked to her about this and established that she would be unwilling to have any blood transfusions or blood products at all administered throughout her pregnancy and birth. This is always worrying as no one knows what is going to happen to any woman throughout this period of time.

I asked her if she would mind seeing a consultant so that her care was managed properly and all risks identified and managed in an appropriate way.

This was accepted and I proceeded with the rest of the booking appointment. Her husband proceeded to inform me that he did not have the same religion as his wife and would find it really difficult to say no if she needed any interventions including blood products if anything went wrong. This is always a difficult situation to be facing but I told the couple, only they could resolve this. They needed to talk about this between themselves and come up with a solution that suited them. I arranged for them to have a scan and took all the necessary blood specimens that were needed. They were advised to make an appointment to see their own midwife when she was 15 weeks pregnant.

I talked to this girl's midwife about her, asking her to make sure she was seen regularly throughout her pregnancy and if she had any problems? I was always happy to talk to her.

Several weeks later, I was contacted by one of the managers and asked if I would take over this lady's care? apparently, the lady and her husband had felt comfortable with me as I was older and they thought wiser. Oh flip, of course I would look after her but hoped that the pregnancy was normal and the baby was born with no problems. I spoke to the other midwife and she was unaware of the request but was happy for me to take over this lady's care, I did say that when I was unavailable, she should work with me and see this lady to make sure all went well. She was agreeable to this and it was left that I would contact her if I was away so that this lady's care was safe.

Unfortunately, this lady had a blood group that was one of the rarer ones. Her blood group was O-Negative. This means that if the baby's father had a positive blood group, the baby could be either negative or positive. If positive, the lady would be offered Anti-D, which stops any positive cells doing any damage to the lady's blood. The lady obviously wanted to decline having the Anti-D, so I suggested that the husband had his blood tested, so that we could determine what his blood group was and to ascertain if they would run into any problems. I explained to them that this would not cause any problems in this current pregnancy but could cause problems in future pregnancies, if the baby had a positive blood group.

The husband agreed to a blood test and attended the ladies next appointment to receive the results. Fortunately, the husband had the same blood group as his wife so this problem was averted. I just hoped that the pregnancy would proceed without any more hiccups. The lady was now 15 weeks pregnant so I was able to listen into the baby's heartbeat for them. Her blood pressure and urine were normal so I arranged to see them after she had her twenty-week scan.

I had a phone call when this lady was 18 weeks pregnant to tell me she had a bleed. I arranged for her to be seen at the hospital to make sure all was well and to reassure them that their baby was doing well. I told her that the midwife would talk to her about having Anti D, as this was always offered when a lady with a Rhesus Negative Blood type had a bleed. I had put the husband's blood results in her notes so told her she should point these out if there were any worries from the staff.

Fortunately, the baby was fine and the bleeding soon stopped. They told me that they had a run in with a midwife who was concerned about her not having Anti D, but a doctor had confirmed that this was not necessary, so she had been sent for a scan to see if they could see any blood around the placenta. This was negative so the lady was discharged back to the community. She had a consultant appointment for when she was 24 weeks pregnant.

The rest of this couple's pregnancy went well and she went into labour, when she was 40 weeks pregnant. The labour went well and although she was pushing for two hours, the baby was delivered with no problems. Blood loss was quite heavy after the placenta was delivered, but this soon stopped without any problems.

Cord blood was taken from the baby so that its blood group could be established. This was shown to be O-Negative so fortunately, Anti D was not necessary. The lady and her baby were transferred to the postnatal ward so that they would be looked after and any problems averted.

This lady returned home with her baby two days later and fortunately, did not have any problems so I was able to discharge her on day ten to the care of the health visitor.

I was so pleased this lady got through her pregnancy and delivery without any problems. A few years earlier, a young lass had been admitted to the hospital who was of the same religion. Unfortunately, she had lost her baby but had bled an awful lot and had needed to have a blood transfusion. The lady and her family had declined this and the lady had to be admitted to the Intensive Care Unit as she was really ill. The doctors and midwives spent an awful lot of time and energy on this case and it caused an awful lot of stress to all the staff involved.

This lady was lucky that she survived. She was extremely unwell for a long period of time. She did eventually get well and go home and a couple of years later, had an uneventful pregnancy and was able to take her baby home.

# Diabetes in Pregnancy

There has been an upward trend of ladies getting type 2 diabetes in pregnancy. All ladies are asked to bring a urine specimen to their appointments and this is tested for any infection, protein or sugar. If we find any sugar in the urine, the lady will be asked to have further testing to ascertain if she had diabetes. A lot of ladies are tested at 28 weeks of pregnancy with a glucose tolerance test to see if they have any problems. This consists of starving overnight, drinking only water before the appointment. A blood test is then taken and after this the lady is given a sugary drink and after a time another blood test is taken to see how the lady metabolises the glucose.

If the test is positive, some ladies will be offered medication, some can control the sugar levels by their diet. Other ladies may have to use insulin to control this condition. Most ladies will find that when their baby is delivered, the diabetes will go away. There is some research to say that ladies who have gestational diabetes are more likely to get this type 2 diabetes later in their lives.

I had a lady who was showing sugar in her urine at booking so was offered the above test. The test revealed she had a high blood sugar in this test so was referred to the diabetic midwife to continue her treatment. She was asked to go on medication but declined this and wanted to control the problem with diet. She was a very slender lady who didn't appear to have any excess fat on her body so it was unusual for a lady like this to have the problem. This lady was provided with a blood glucose monitor so that she could check her glucose levels several times a day.

It's quite difficult to bring the blood sugar down by diet, sugar is in an awful lot of foods and fruit contains more sugar than people think. My lady was very diligent in her efforts to maintain her glucose levels. It was not easy but in the most part she succeeded. She cut out most carbohydrates, and limited her fruit intake and eventually delivered a lovely baby who had no problems.

Diabetes can cause lots problems throughout pregnancy and birth. Babies can be much bigger than normal and can be difficult to deliver. The baby once delivered can have low blood sugars after the birth and needs to be checked on a regular basis. They are also more likely to have abnormalities, so it is really important that these ladies are seen regularly throughout their pregnancies so that problems are minimised and the outcome is good for both mother and baby.

# Bicornuate Uterus

I booked a lady who had a Bicornuate Uterus. This means she had a uterus that was split into two, she also had two cervix and two vaginas. She knew this because she had problems with her periods where she was bleeding constantly and had been sent to a gynaecologist. He had sent her for a scan and this was how it was diagnosed.

It was thought that this lady may have problems conceiving but fortunately, she got pregnant quite quickly after trying.

The booking visit went well and she and her husband were happy to see a consultant to make sure that she was carefully monitored during her pregnancy.

I did tell her that she was quite likely to deliver early as having this condition usual meant that the smaller uterus did not stretch as much as a normal size uterus would. It's difficult to say when she would deliver, but usually it's any time after 34 weeks. I told her that nearer to the time, I would arrange for her to go and look around the special care baby unit so that they felt more comfortable with their baby having to go there for a time if this happened. I also told them that this may not happen, but it was best to be prepared.

The lady was also told that the baby would be in one horn (side) of the uterus and that she may still have periods from the other uterus. I told her that this may not happen but it's always best to be aware of this.

I booked this lady for a scan and arranged to see her when she was 15 weeks pregnant. She was given telephone numbers so that she could ring me if she was worried.

When the lady had her scan, she rang me to tell me she was expecting twins, one in each horn of the uterus. This is extremely rare and after congratulations, I arranged to see her the next week. I was shown the scan result and it showed she had a baby in each horn of the uterus and it was shown from the scan that each baby had been conceived at different times. One baby was the right size for her dates. The other was over two weeks behind in growth. I was able to hear both heartbeats which really made the lady and her husband happy. I tried to reassure them that they would be well looked after and all precautions for the safe arrival of their babies would be taken.

The lady's pregnancy went well until she was 30 weeks, then her waters went and she was admitted to the hospital for observation. Two days later, it was decided that this lady needed to be delivered as her blood pressure was getting out of control and she was suffering from 'preeclampsia' (a disorder of pregnancy that can cause problems for the mother and the baby. The only way to cure this is to deliver the baby). She was given medication to bring down her blood pressure but this was not helping. She was prepared for a caesarean section and taken to theatre.

Both babies were born alive and both cried lustfully so this was good news for the couple. One baby was 3 lbs and the other one was 2 lbs 9 oz. They were both taken to the special care baby unit and needed help with their breathing for the first week of their lives. They then did very well. I am always happy when its girls that are born that early, they nearly always do better than boys, no one seems to know why this is the case but it's true.

I visited the babies on the unit and kept in contact with the family until both babies were able to be discharged home. They were seven weeks old when they went home and both did very well. It was a great outcome and the parents were great and coped with it all really well. It was lovely to see them altogether at home after such a long time.

# Terrible Headache

One of my ladies had been discharged from hospital the day before after giving birth to a baby girl. When I arrived at the house, I was met by a husband who was very worried about his wife. I was asked to go upstairs to the bedroom to see her and her baby. The poor girl was very tearful and was obviously in pain. I gave her a hug and sat down to listen to what was happening to her.

I asked her about her birth and was told she had been in labour a long time and was offered an epidural for pain relief. She had accepted this and had found it very beneficial. The baby had been born with the help of forceps and everything had been fine. The problem had started the next morning when she had been complaining of a headache. She was assured that this was normal and that the headache would resolve on its own.

Unfortunately, this had not happened and it was clear that she had what is called Postural Headache. This meant that when she was lying flat, she was fine but when she tried to sit up, the pain was unbearable.

I knew from her symptoms that she had a post-epidural headache. This does happen rarely and it is very incapacitating. Sometimes these headaches resolve, but it was clear that this lady needed treating.

I rang the hospital and spoke to one of the senior staff who kindly said that the lady should be sent to the delivery suite so that she could be treated.

I explained to the couple what had happened and how this would be treated. When an epidural is sited, rarely the dura membrane is hit and this causes terrible headaches as the spinal fluid is escaping through this hole. The resolution to this is for an anaesthetist to use the patient's own blood to patch the hole. This makes the headache go away and the problem is resolved.

I reassured them that this would be done today and she would immediately feel better. The lady was too uncomfortable to be transferred to hospital by car, so I called an ambulance who could of course take her in whilst lying flat. The couple agreed to this and I waited until the ambulance came and then told her I would see her in the hospital the next morning or at home if she was discharged by then.

This lady was taken to theatre and had a blood patch to resolve the problem. Thankfully, this had made the headache go away and the lady was better. She was taken to the postnatal ward for the night and was well enough to be discharged the next morning.

It was lovely to see the lady at home with her baby and minus a headache. She had no further problems and I was able to discharge her when the baby was ten days old.

# A Strange Booking

A lady came for a booking appointment for her second baby. This would be her second child. She had a three nearly four-year-old boy who came to the appointment with her. I had not met this lady before as she had moved area since her first delivery, so introduced myself and told her what would happen during the appointment.

The lady had one request before I started the booking. She handed me a piece of paper saying she did not want her child to know she was pregnant, so wanted me to resist from mentioning babies during the appointment.

I told her this was fine, so continued with the appointment. The first question that is usually asked is where they would like to have their baby. I got round this by asking where she wanted her offspring to be born to which she answered I don't know what you mean. Not a good start, so I reworded it by asking where would you like to labour. Fortunately, she realised what I was asking and told me she would like me to book her for the local hospital.

The rest of the booking was completed and I arranged to see her when she was 15 weeks pregnant. A scan appointment was arranged, bloods were taken as usual.

The next time I met this lady was when she attended for her next appointment. She told me she was well and her scan had gone well. Her blood pressure and urine were normal and I then asked the lady if she would like me to have a listen. She had her son with her and had already informed me that he still was unaware of the situation, so she asked me if I would listen in but not tell her son what was going on.

I listened in to the baby and the son was of course curious. I said to him that mummy had rice crispies for breakfast and I was seeing if I could hear them in her tummy. This seemed to satisfy both of them but I must admit I did wonder when the child was going to be told of the pregnancy. Obviously, this was up to the parents and it was difficult to discuss this with her with her son in the room but I thought once the pregnancy was showing then he would be told.

How wrong I was? I saw this lady regularly throughout her pregnancy and she always attended with her son. This lady was 36 weeks pregnant and she still had not told her son. I arranged to do a home visit the next week to discuss the birth and hoped that she would discuss with me about why she was keeping the pregnancy from her son? Just before she left the surgery, her son was playing and touched the side of the sharps box, which was on the side beside the sink. I moved it out of his way and as he had not put his hand into the sharps box as he couldn't reach it, I was not worried about this.

The next day I had a phone call from the lady who was worried about the sharps box. I told her that he had not touched the inside of the box as he could not reach it, so I was not worried. I took the opportunity to ask the lady when she intended to inform her child of the upcoming birth and was told that she intended to leave it until they bought the baby home.

The child by this time was four, so I must admit I was slightly surprised about this decision, but it was their decision. I hoped the parents bringing a baby home would not be too much of a shock to their son.

I spoke to the lady's GP about the situation, the birth and also what had happened about the sharps box. The GP was surprised they had not told their son but told me that the lady had always been anxious about things and agreed with me that we should keep a close eye on her and try to support her as much as we could.

I attended her home for a discussion about the birth and fortunately her son was at his grandma's house, so I could be quite open with her. We discussed what she wanted to happen during her birth and what pain relief she would like. After this discussion, I asked her when she and her husband were going to tell their son about the imminent birth. She told me that they still wanted to keep it a secret until the baby was born and they bought it home. She told me that she did not want her son to visit her in the hospital as she thought this would distress him.

It is always up to the parents when they inform their children about a new baby, but I wondered what the child thought about his mum's baby bump, and also the amount of rice crispies she appeared to have eaten before I listened in to the baby.

This lady had friends who were pregnant with their second child and had met with some of them throughout her pregnancy, so I actually wonder if her son already knew what was happening. His friends would I have thought, talked about their mummies bumps and the baby that was in their tummies. I just hoped that the child would not be too upset about the upcoming event.

This lady delivered naturally at 40 weeks. She was discharged from hospital the next day and I visited her the following day.

The birth had gone well and her baby girl was beautiful. I was hoping that the family were now all home together and that the older child was not too surprised that he now had a sister.

I arrived at the house and was invited in. Their son was with his father when he came to the door, so I said hello have you got something to show me? He took me by the hand and proceeded to show me a new car his granny had bought him. I said to him a little bird told me that you have a new sister. Yes he said, mummy and daddy went shopping for her yesterday. Oh well that's one way of putting it.

The lady and her baby did well and I only heard the son say on one occasion, can you take her back to the shop she makes too much noise. Oh dear, that's a difficult one to answer.

# Rude Husbands

I booked a lady for a home birth. She was having her second baby and had a normal birth with her first child. She was a lovely lady and her little boy was delightful. The booking went well and all her checks were normal. Bloods were taken and I arranged to see her at 15 weeks. I gave her information about home births and asked if her husband was in agreement with this. I was told that he was up for it as he hadn't enjoyed the hospital experience with their first child.

I saw this lady regularly throughout her pregnancy and she had no problems at all. The baby grew well and I arranged to see her at home when she was 36 weeks to discuss the home birth. I told the lady that I was happy to do this on weekends, so that her husband was around and he could voice any concerns he had.

The day of the assessment arrived. I arrived at the house and was invited in. The husband was sitting in the living room on the computer and although I said hello, he completely ignored me. I was talking to the lady about what she would need for the delivery and what we would bring with us. I tried to bring her husband into the conversation but he just carried on with what he was doing. I was quite surprised by this as the lady did not say anything to him at all. I must admit I thought it was a bit odd and slightly rude.

After the assessment, I arranged to see the lady the next week in clinic and said goodbye to her and her silent husband feeling quite uncomfortable about the way he had behaved. All people are different so I just put it down to a different experience.

I have always tried to deliver my own ladies although, sometimes this has not happened. This lady went into labour when I was available so I drove to her house at around 1 am one Sunday morning.

Arriving at the house, I was invited into the lounge by the lady and offered a cup of tea. I accepted and began asking her about her labour. She told me she had been in labour for four hours and the contractions were coming every three to four minutes and were lasting about forty seconds. I took her blood pressure, temperature and pulse which were all normal. An examination of her cervix found her to be 7 cm dilated. This was really good, and I told her how well she was doing.

I then asked her where her husband was? I was informed he was asleep in bed. This was followed by the comment he gets a bit grumpy when he is tired. Poor thing. I admit I felt like saying to her get him up he should be here supporting you at this time. I did ask her when she intended to wake him up and was told she would leave him until she was fully dilated.

This was a first, for nearly all the home births I have attended, I have found the dads to be very supportive and willing to help during this important time so was a bit taken aback by this attitude.

The labour was progressing quite quickly, so I told the lady I was calling the second midwife to give her a chance to get to us in time as she lived quite a way from the hospital. The lady agreed with this and I got everything ready for the birth. The baby's heartbeat remained steady and her blood pressure was good. She was coping beautifully and was totally relaxed.

Sometime later, the lady was feeling pressure in her bottom so I told her it was time to wake her husband. She agreed it was and she went upstairs to wake him. At that point the second midwife arrived, so I let her in and updated her as to what was happening. She was quite surprised also about the husband situation, but as I said it takes all sorts to make the world go round.

The lady came downstairs and told us her husband was awake and would join us in a few minutes.

A few minutes later, the husband appeared and we both greeted him and told him how well his wife was doing. His answer was a grunt and good, I need to get back to bed I am tired. Oh well, that was us told.

A short time later, the lady wanted to push. I told her to do what her body was telling her to do. She did this beautifully and within minutes she had delivered her baby. I handed her the baby and she cuddled her to her chest and was obviously delighted. Congratulations were given and the husbands reply was I am going back to bed, I am tired. I must admit I was shocked. I told him that she would need help and support for the next few hours and could he stay up to support her. He obviously wasn't very happy with this but he grunted and sat down on the sofa and from what I could see sulked.

The placenta was delivered and the lady did not need any stitches. We made her comfortable on the sofa with the baby and offered to make her a cup of tea. I must admit I was ready for one too. The other midwife made her way to the kitchen, the husband shouted after her, make mine a coffee and don't make a mess. How rude is that? I looked at him and thought to myself, he needed to get off his backside and make himself useful but this obviously was not going to happen.

The notes were completed and the lady had a shower. The baby was checked and weighed and dressed and put into the Moses basket. The lady was taken up to her room and tucked into bed and we left her with telephone numbers she could ring if she had any problems. The baby had already breastfed so she was happy when we told her that she would be visited by a midwife that afternoon. The lady thanked us for letting her have such a lovely delivery and we told her we were very happy for her and how well she had done.

We went downstairs to say goodbye to the husband, who was settled on the sofa. He grunted and told us he was going to sleep on the settee as he did not want to be disturbed by the baby. I was actually quite shocked and asked him if he was able to take any time off work to help his wife with the baby and toddler. He told me he had a very important job and was unable to do this. I asked him if either of their mothers could come and help and was told that he hadn't asked them. My suggestion was that they talked between them and get some help for his wife.

We left the house after packing all the equipment away, with no help from the husband and we both felt that he was not the most supportive or helpful husband we had ever come across and he was actually quite rude. I have never before met a husband like this at a home birth and actually felt quite sorry for the lady. It takes two to make a baby and it takes two to look after it. Usually couples are so excited about the birth of their baby. The lady was obviously delighted but the husband's reaction was quite different.

I visited this lady the following day and she was doing well. Fortunately, her mother had come to stay and support her so she had plenty of help. The lady apologised about the way her husband had acted and told me he was good with the other child, when he had enough sleep but was quite grumpy when he was tired. She was right. He did and acted like a petulant child but it was not my place to point this out.

I saw this lady regularly until I discharged her but never came face to face with her husband again. I do hope when her mother went home, he would step up to the plate and help out with his wife and the children. I informed the health visitor of the situation and she said she would keep an eye on her and give her the support she needed.

# Busy Clinic

It was my usual clinic day and the clinic was full and overflowing. The first lady was a booking a first-time mum who had come with her mother. I talked to her about the pregnancy and asked her where she wanted to deliver? Her mother told me she wanted her to deliver at a hospital which was many miles from our area but the girl herself wanted to deliver at the local hospital. I agreed to this and carried on with the booking. The history became quite prolonged as the girl's mother kept interrupting and disagreeing with what she was telling me. I must admit I found it a bit frustrating but carried on regardless. Bloods were discussed and taken and her urine was tested and found to be normal. I talked to the girl about her diet and things she should avoid much to the mother's disgust. She told me she had eaten normally during her pregnancy and thought it was ridiculous information I was giving her daughter.

I informed the girl and her mother that she could look on the NHS website to give her further information on her diet and pregnancy and this was greeted with, well we didn't need websites when I was pregnant. Well, fortunately times have changed and much more is known these days about what is good for ladies and their babies.

I arranged to see the lady when she was 15 weeks pregnant and arranged for her to have a scan. The mother was asking me why I hadn't arranged for her daughter to see a consultant? I told her that everything was very normal at the moment and if things changed at all, she would be referred to see a consultant.

I must admit, I felt exhausted when they left and I had a long afternoon ahead of me.

The next lady arrived and fortunately had no problems, so I was relieved that everything was normal and after doing her check she left happily.

The next few patients were all normal and left happily. Then a lady arrived with her partner who was obviously very into the pregnancy. He was a delightful chap and was very interested in what was going on. He kept asking. When will you listen in to the baby's heartbeat? I reassured him that after checking her blood pressure and urine, we would listen to the heartbeat. Bless him, he was on the edge of his seat and was obviously very excited with what was going on.

The time had come and after measuring the size of the uterus, I listened in to the heartbeat. The husband was beside himself and wanted to ring his parents and his friends so they could listen in too. I suggested that he should record the heartbeat on his mobile phone so that he could listen and share with whoever he wanted too. This was accepted and after checking that it had recorded properly, they left very happily.

This clinic seemed endless. I had already seen twelve ladies and had several more who were due to arrive.

The last lady due to arrive was always late for her appointment. Fortunately, I was running slightly late so I would not have to hang around waiting for her. I admit when patients are always late for their appointments, it makes me a little annoyed. The lady concerned came late to every appointment with no apologies but informing me that she had a very high-powered job and it was extremely difficult for her to get away.

Finally, the last appointment slot and the lady had not arrived. I started clearing up around me and although it was thirty minutes after her appointment time, the lady arrived and I heard the receptionist say to her I will ask the midwife if she can see you, you are very late for your appointment. To this the lady replied – well, I have an important job and find it difficult to get away.

The receptionist rang through to me and I said I would see her but I was really a bit miffed that she was so late. I invited her in and I was able to check her over. All was well and as the lady was 36 weeks pregnant, I asked her when she was going to take maternity leave? I was informed that she was working until she delivered and was taking a month off work.

I was slightly surprised by this but everyone is different. I did say to the lady that if she had a caesarean section, she would not be able to return to work for up to six weeks as this was considered a major operation.

Just before I had finished the consultation, I asked her to make an appointment in two weeks. The lady left and I tidied up the room and was able to leave for home.

The receptionist told me that the lady who had come late for her appointment had asked for the last appointment of the clinic when she had made her appointment. This appointment had already been taken so she was given an earlier appointment and told that she should be on time as otherwise it put the entire clinic late. She told the receptionist that she would attend as near to the appointment time as she could, but sometimes it was difficult for her to get away.

I must admit I am always early for appointments; I can't stand to be late for anything and actually think it is disrespectful to the person you are seeing. Most of my ladies were great with their appointment times and if they are held up, they always ring ahead and let us know. Maybe I expect too much.

The lady concerned actually delivered at 39 weeks, she had a long labour and had unfortunately had a caesarean section. I saw her at home afterwards and she was doing very well. I talked to her about her work plans and advised her to try to take at least six weeks off to give herself time to heal. I was surprised when she told me she was already answering emails from her place of work and had several phone calls asking her for information. Apparently, she had several phone calls whilst she was still in the hospital.

This lady's baby was four days old, so I thought this was a bit much and not fair of her colleagues to be using her in this way so soon after the birth.

I visited this lady regularly and was able to discharge her on day ten. She told me she was intending to go to work when the baby was a month old. I told her that she should inform her insurance company that she would be driving before the six week period suggested after a caesarean section. Most insurance companies are fine as long as they have been informed and that the lady is fit to drive with permission from her GP or midwife.

I have only come across this once before. I visited a lady for a colleague and the husband was at home with the baby and informed me that his wife had gone to work. The baby was three days old, so I was somewhat surprised. I told him that it was important that his wife was checked over by a midwife and would it be possible for her to stay at home the next day until the midwife had been.

The husband told me that this would not be possible and that his wife worked twelve-hour shifts and would not be home until after 10 pm and could the midwife visit her then. Urgh, no that's not something we would be able to do. He went on to say, well don't you have midwives on duty overnight? I informed him that we do have midwives on call from 9 pm but as I explained to him a visit at that time of the evening would be not be classed as an emergency and the hospital would have to pay the midwife overtime for attending. This overnight service is for home births and any emergencies that occur.

I told her husband that I could arrange for her to be seen at the weekend clinic during the day. The answer to this was well she works the weekends as well. I asked him which days off she had and was told that she worked six days a week so on her day off, would not want to go to the hospital.

I checked the baby over and he was doing very well, he was bottle feeding well, his colour was good and was filling his nappy appropriately.

The husband was informed that I would ask the midwife who was on over the weekend to arrange a visit but he should not be surprised if he got a phone call asking them to attend the weekend clinic.

Women are given maternity leave to enable them to rest and recover from their birth and to give them time to bond with their baby. Most women need this time to recover and enjoy their time off. I cannot understand women who have babies and return to work immediately. It takes all sorts to make the world go round. Personally, I don't know how they cope with the night feeds, the lack of sleep and extra work that a baby entails.

# From Immaculate to Dirty

I was visiting a lady for another midwife who was on holiday. I arrived at the house and was invited in. When I go into other people's houses, I always ask if they want me to take my shoes off. In this house I didn't. The place was filthy. The floors were so dirty, my shoes were sticking to the carpet. I put my jacket on the chair I was offered as it was extremely dirty.

The lady and her husband were lovely and offered me a drink which I quickly declined! They were so excited with their new baby and he was doing really well. The lady was breastfeeding which I was pleased to see as I didn't know how the sterilization of bottles would be carried out in this house.

This couple were so friendly and didn't seem a bit bothered about the state of their house. I could have written my name in the dust around the living room and the smell was pretty awful, but they seemed really happy with their lot.

I must admit when I went to wash my hands, I dried them on my cardigan. The smell in the kitchen was horrendous and I admit I was very happy when I was able to leave.

Later that morning, I visited a house in a very different area. The house was huge, the gardens were lovely and I wasn't quite sure which front door bell to press. One was for visitors; another was for workmen. I pressed the visitor bell and the door was opened by a lady who introduced herself as the housekeeper. I informed her I was the midwife and had come to see the lady and her baby.

I was invited in and I immediately took off my shoes. They had white carpets and before I could speak, the housekeeper asked me to stay where I was until she had informed the lady of the house that I had arrived.

I stood where I was for about ten minutes until the housekeeper reappeared. She had some plastic sheeting with her and informed me she had to lay it on the carpet as my feet were possibly dirty.

I suppressed a laugh and told her they were very clean and I wouldn't dream of walking on the white carpet in my shoes. I did as I was told and stood where I was until the lady had placed her plastic sheeting on the floor. There was part of me that wanted to say will you hurry up? I have other visits to do but I decided to keep quiet and go with the flow.

Eventually, I was allowed to go into the very big front room where I met the lady and her baby. I introduced myself and was greeted with the lady saying that it was very inconvenient for me to be there then as she was expecting visitors. My reply was, I am sorry but I have a clinic to do this afternoon so it was now or nothing.

The lady then remarked that I should hurry up as she didn't want her friends arriving whilst I was still there. What a cheek. I asked her for her notes and was not invited to sit down. In fact, I was asked to stay where I was as I was told I could bring other people's dirt into her house!!

The notes were given to me and I asked her how the feeding was going? She told me that the baby was bottle fed and she had a night nurse who was looking after the baby during the night hours. The baby looked well and I asked if I could wash my hands before I handled her? The housekeeper was asked to bring a bowl, soap and towel in so I could do this. I must admit, I was a bit shocked especially when I had washed my hands and dried them, the housekeeper was told to sterilize the bowl and put the towel in the washing machine.

The lady told me she was fine and the only problem she had was that her breasts were extremely painful. This happens to most ladies on day three and I reassured her that this would get better over the next few days. I was asked if she could have an injection to resolve this problem. I told her that it wasn't common practise to do this as the problem would resolve over the next few days. This was met with her telling me she would ask her private doctor to provide this injection for her.

When the visit was over, I told the lady that a midwife would visit her in two days to see how she and her baby were doing and I left her with phone numbers so she could contact us if she had any problems.

I was quite relieved when the visit was over and I could make my way to my own clinic. I was telling the receptionists about my morning and they were indignant about the way the Posh lady had treated me. I laughed and told them it was fine and hopefully I would not be asked to go there again. I did tell them that the lady would have been horrified if she knew I had been in a filthy house before I visited her. It takes all sorts to make the world go around and the majority of the ladies I visit, were nice normal clean people who were always pleased to see the midwife and very appreciative of our care and visits.

# Another Call Out, Another Home Birth

Once again the phone rang in the middle of the night and I was called to a home birth. I made my way to the house and hoped it would be a nice easy birth, with a lovely couple and no dramas.

I arrived at the house and was invited in. This was a couple who were having their first child. They had a nice normal pregnancy and were hoping for a water birth. We had a chat about how things were going and what they wanted from the birth.

I examined the lady and her blood pressure was slightly elevated but all the other recordings were good. She was 5 cm dilated and was having contractions every three minutes. The baby's heartbeat was regular and she was coping very well. I informed the lady about her elevated blood pressure and told her we would keep an eye on it and hopefully it would settle, if it continued to be elevated we would have to think about going to the hospital for the safety of the mum and the baby.

The couple were happy with this plan and we settled down with a nice cup of tea to await events. Fortunately, the blood pressure was normal the next time I checked it and I told the lady I must have frightened her when I first took it to which she laughed and said she was quite apprehensive that she wasn't in labour and that I would tell her nothing was happening and I wasn't going to stay. I told the couple that I was staying and would keep an eye on her blood pressure regularly to make sure it was behaving.

This lady was great, she was so relaxed and coped beautifully with the contractions. In fact, she was so controlled it was difficult to know if she was contracting or not.

Her husband was busy getting the pool ready and the lady was very relieved when she could get in and use the pool for relaxation and pain relief.

The labour was going well and she was great, she breathed quietly throughout her contractions and fortunately her blood pressure remained low. The baby's heartbeat was regular and the pool temperature was well controlled.

After a few hours of this, the lady told me that she could feel pressure and that she started to feel that she was not coping very well. I offered her the gas and air which she was happy to use and found it very helpful. I told her that I was going to call the hospital for the second midwife to attend as she was progressing so well.

The lady was worried that she wasn't dilating and I told her it was highly unlikely with all the contractions she had throughout her labour, but I offered to examine her cervix to reassure her if she needed that.

We discussed this and I told her that I was happy not to examine her, but would willingly do so if she felt she needed confirmation that things were progressing. The couple told me they thought that she needed examining every few hours to see if she was continuing to progress. I reassured them that when I could see she was doing well and the baby was happy it was not imperative that this happened.

Whilst we were discussing this, she told me she needed to push to which I replied great, just do what your body tells you to do. The second midwife was called and the lady stayed in the pool pushing with each contraction.

I placed a mirror on the bottom of the pool so that progress could be seen and told the lady I could see the baby's head. At that moment, the doorbell rang and the second midwife came into the room. I updated her on what was happening and a few minutes later, the baby's head delivered. I asked the lady not to push until the baby had got itself into a position so that its shoulders and body could be delivered.

The lady was so compliant, she breathed for a couple of minutes and then told me she needed to push, so I encouraged her to do this and a beautiful baby girl was born and put into the delighted mother's arms. The couple were absolutely delighted with the baby and asked what they needed to do next.

It was decided that she would get out of the pool to deliver the placenta, so the cord was clamped and cut by the husband and the baby was given to the daddy and the lady was got out of the pool onto the sofa.

The lady asked me if she had to have the injection to help deliver the afterbirth, I told her that she didn't have to have it and we should wait and see if the placenta would deliver on its own. If this seemed to be delayed, then she could have the injection. This was agreed and about five minutes later, the lady told me she had a pain and felt pressure so I encouraged her to push and the placenta was delivered.

The couple were delighted with their delivery and their beautiful baby and were elated that all had gone well. No stitches were needed and the baby was given to the mum and put to the breast so that she could feed. Fortunately, this happened quickly and it was decided that we should celebrate with a nice cup of tea.

For a first-time mum, this lady had done extremely well. She was calm, relaxed and very open to suggestions to help her on her way. I told them they had been a delight to look after and they could have a home birth as often as they liked.

The room was cleared, the pool was drained and the notes were filled in and after making sure the lady had a bath and made comfortable in bed we left to go back to the hospital to fill in the notes and to restock the bags.

Telephone numbers were left with the couple and we arranged for a midwife to visit them that afternoon.

We left a very happy family behind us and after going back to the hospital, we were able to go home to our beds.

# A Delivery with the Bailiffs

Many years ago when I was a young midwife, I was called to a home birth in the middle of the night. When I arrived, I was invited in to a very strange household.

The lady and her partner lived in a flat in a shared house. They had a shared bathroom with several other families and the flat was very sparce in the furnishing department. They had a bed, one chair and bare floorboards. They shared a kitchen and bathroom with the other families, which were on another floor of the building.

The couple were lovely and were very excited to be having a baby. The lady was five days overdue and had been contracting for several hours.

I did all the regular checks and the baby was happy and mum was doing and coping very well. I phoned the hospital and updated them with what was happening and sat back (on the floor) to await events.

Contractions were coming regularly and all seemed to be well. The lady was 6 cm dilated when I had examined her, so I was hoping that the labour would not last too many hours.

As I was a fairly new midwife at the time, a second midwife had been asked to attend to back me up. I must admit, I was quite pleased when she arrived. I had not met this midwife before but I had heard about her. She was very particular in her ways and if she didn't like what was going on, she would say so.

The midwife arrived and immediately told me she didn't like the fact that I was sitting on the floor, she thought it was unprofessional.

I must admit it wasn't very comfortable sitting on the bare floorboards, but other than standing up for hours there was not much I could do about it. I did use my coat as a cushion.

Sometime later, dawn was breaking and the lady told me she wanted to push. I encouraged her to do what her body was telling her to do. The older midwife tutted and said balderdash. If she is fully dilated, she needs to push and just get on with it.

It's really difficult when you are newly trained and a midwife who had many years of experience tells you that you need to what I think is bully the lady into pushing. I spoke to the lady quietly and just encouraged her to push if she had the urge. Fortunately, the urge came quite quickly so she started pushing with each contraction and was doing very well.

Just as the baby's head became visible, there was a loud knocking at the front door of the house. Obviously, we ignored it as we were busy delivering a baby.

The baby's head was born when there was a knock at the couple's door. The other midwife shouted, "We are busy, come back later!"

Just as the baby was being born, two burly men who told us they were bailiffs pushed the door in and entered the room. At the time, we obviously didn't know what they wanted, but to say we were shocked is an understatement.

The two men stood at the door and said you have an hour to vacate the room. I just turned around and said do you really think this lady can leave in that time? she has just delivered her first baby.

We were bluntly told, "It's not our problem, we have been sent to move everyone out of all the rooms in the house."

It appeared that the person who said he owned the house had lied and was letting out rooms to six different families, but had not had permission to let out the rooms as he was a tenant and was subletting illegally.

This put us in a really difficult position. The poor lady had not even delivered the placenta, so there was no way she could be thrown into the street. I tried to reason with the bailiffs but they were not having it. They did say they would give the lady time to deliver the placenta before they chucked her out. The bailiffs left the room to deal with the other families concerned.

Obviously they were very distressed, so I discussed this with the couple and asked them if they had any family they could go and stay with until they could find another property to rent or be able to go to the council to try and get some help.

The other midwife was jumping up and down following the men out of the room and telling the bailiffs they could not treat the couple like this but unfortunately, this fell on deaf ears. The midwife returned to the room and the air was blue.

The lady said they could go and stay with her parents, but they were away until the weekend which was three days away.

I suggested to the lady that we transfer her to the hospital so that she could be looked after whilst her partner tried to sort the problem out. The other midwife was not happy with this but as I said we could not see her evicted onto the street when she had just given birth. Fortunately, after a few choice words she agreed with me and after we discussed it with the couple an ambulance was called to transport her to the hospital.

Soon after this, the placenta was delivered and fortunately the lady did not need any stitches. I felt so sorry for this couple. The husband was quickly trying to pack all their belongings before they were asked to leave. Fortunately, they had not got much to be packed up but as the couple did not have a car, he had nowhere to put it whilst he accompanied his wife to the hospital.

I had never before or since been in this position, it's a really difficult dilemma, I can understand why the owner of the house wanted it back, but there were six families who were being evicted with nowhere to go.

The noise coming from the other occupants of the house was awful, obviously they were all unhappy with what was going on and were understandably furious about being chucked out of their rooms especially at 7 am in the morning.

The ambulance arrived to take this lady to the maternity unit and they agreed to take the suitcases the husband had packed with them, so that they didn't lose their belongings. They were told that they could fetch the other things left in the house within a week.

The outcome to this lady's birth was that she stayed in the hospital for three days. She then went home to her mother's house. Her partner went to the council and fortunately they helped and could put them in temporary accommodation until they were able to find a house for them.

I managed to visit this lady after she had her baby and although they were very unhappy with the way they had been evicted, they felt happy that they would be getting a council house. They didn't know what had happened to the other people who lived in the house and apparently when the partner went back to the house to collect their belongings, they were all thrown in the garden. Thank goodness, it had not rained. They were enjoying their new baby and her parents had welcomed them into their house, which made it much better for them.

I have never been put in this position before and hope it never happens to anyone else in the middle of labour.

# Poorly Baby

One of my ladies who lived in a small village had delivered and was due a visit from me. I arrived at her house at about lunchtime and was welcomed in.

The lady told me that the baby was really good and had not woken up in the night at all for a feed. She had breastfed for a few minutes that morning but was really sleepy. This was their first baby so they just thought that they had a well-behaved baby. My immediate thought was oh no, this doesn't sound good.

We went up to the baby's nursery and I was quite shocked by the baby's colour. She was pale and just lay in her cot. I washed my hands and then lifted the baby out of her cot to examine her. I could tell straight away that she was a very sick baby, she was pale and quite limp. Her skin was blotchy and she really looked unwell. Her nappy was dry and it turned out that no urine had been seen overnight.

The baby's temperature was low and I quickly realised that this baby needed to be transferred into the hospital. I explained this to the parents and called an ambulance. The parents were obviously upset but I assured them that the baby would be in the best place to get better and that mum and dad would be able to stay at the hospital if they wanted too.

The ambulance arrived quickly and the paramedics were great. They realised that the baby was very poorly and were quick in taking the baby and the mum to the hospital. The husband decided to drive in his car so that he could have time to pack a bag and inform their parents what was happening. I told them that I would ring the hospital later to see what was happening and would visit them in the hospital in the morning.

I rang the hospital later that day and found out that the baby had been diagnosed with meningitis. I was so pleased that I had not been too late in the day visiting the couple and the baby had reached the hospital in good time.

The next morning I went to the special care baby unit to visit the baby. She was on intravenous antibiotics and thankfully was improving. Her temperature was now normalising, she was having her feeds by a nasogastric (nasal) tube and was awake when I saw her. The parents were both in the ward with her and had been given a bedroom in the ward behind the unit which was kept solely for use of parents, whose baby were on the special care baby unit.

I checked mum over and she was doing well, she was obviously upset that her baby was ill but thankful that she was improving. I arranged to see her the next day on the ward and told her she could ring me if she had any worries.

This baby was on the ward for a week and then was transferred home. The parents were anxious that this would happen again and needed reassurance that this was highly unlikely. We would visit daily for a few days until they got their confidence back.

The outcome of this was that the baby did very well. Mum managed to breastfeed her and I was able to discharge her when the baby was three weeks old.

My eldest daughter Charlotte had viral meningitis when she was sixteen. She had been complaining of not feeling well for a few days but had been taking exams, so I had put it down to stress. That was a mistake.

The following weekend I was working, so left for work and Charlotte was still in bed when I left. A few hours later, my husband rang and told me that she was really poorly and I should go home and see what I thought.

I rang my colleagues and returned home to find a daughter who had lost some of the feeling in her legs, her temperature was high and she was obviously not well at all.

I rang the surgery and they told me to take her down so we put her in the car and drove her to the surgery. We were seen immediately and the doctor said she thought she needed to go to accident and emergency.

We went to the hospital and almost carried her into the department. We were taken straight through to a room and a doctor saw her and thought she had meningitis. I was so shocked, and terrified. I had seen the outcome of meningitis.

She was transferred to a ward and Richard went home as we had left our other daughter Emma on her own. She was 14 at the time but was obviously upset by what had happened.

I stayed with Charlotte and she was seen by several doctors. She was to have a lumber puncture (a needle into the spine to extract fluid). I was ushered out of the room until this had been done. Unfortunately, the doctors had to try several times before they were able to access the spinal fluid.

Sometime later, a doctor approached me and said well she either has meningitis or a brain tumour. I nearly fell to the ground. The sister came up and asked me if I was okay as unsurprisingly I had turned a shade of green. The doctor told her what he had told me and she said to him do you realise this is the girl's mother? Apparently, he thought I was staff as I was still wearing my uniform.

He apologised and told me that she was being given all the treatment she needed and that I should go home and return in the morning. I told him I was not going anywhere and would stay with Charlotte in her room. He shrugged and said it's up to you and walked out of the ward.

The sister was lovely. She told me that she thought that it was unlikely to be a brain tumour and was probably viral meningitis and that she would slowly improve.

Thankfully, she was right. Charlotte improved slowly and was discharged home some ten days later. I was shocked when her exam results came through that she had done so well, as she had done her exams holding her head up by her hand. I felt so guilty that I had thought she was just feeling stressed. Her diagnosis was viral meningitis which is the better one to have if you have to have it. She slowly got better over the holidays and was ready to go back to school after the holidays.

# Smelly Nappies

I was in the middle of my clinic and a lady who had a booking appointment came in with her young son. I introduced myself and she told me she was eight weeks pregnant and her son was seven months old. This pregnancy was a surprise but she was very happy and looking forward to having another baby.

I went through the notes with her and heard an explosion from her baby son. He had obviously filled his nappy and it stank. Oh my goodness. I told her I was happy for her to change his nappy so that he was more comfortable. She was happy to do this and whilst she was doing this, I asked her what she fed her baby as the smell was so awful.

She told me that he had had a McDonald's meal the day before, and she had whizzed it up for him as she wanted to feed her son the same food as she and her partner ate. She went on to tell me that her baby had enjoyed his big mac.

To say I was surprised was an understatement. Usually, mums feed their babies mashed up fruit or vegetables. I didn't know this lady so I didn't want to hurt her feelings, but I did ask her, have you seen the health visitor since you moved to the area.

This hadn't happened but I told her I would let the health visitor know that she had recently moved into the area.

Unfortunately, the nappy was still in the room so the smell was still wafting through the room.

I continued with the appointment and referred the lady to see a consultant as she had told me she delivered her son at 34 weeks. She said her waters had gone and she had been 8 cm dilated when she arrived at the hospital. It was not known why she had delivered early as she had no signs of infection and the baby had weighed 5 lbs so he was a really good size for his dates.

After I had finished her notes and taken her blood sample, I arranged to see her when she was 15 weeks pregnant.

When she left the room, I had to go in search of an air freshener, the windows were flung open and I also had to remove the nappy from the bin and put it in the bin outside the building. I could almost taste the smell, it was horrendous. I hoped that after a visit from the health visitor, she would get some help with what to feed her son.

When the lady was 15 weeks pregnant I saw her at the clinic and she was well. Her son was with her and I was hoping he would save his bowel movement until she had left the room.

During the consultation, I asked her if she had met with the health visitor and she had. She had been given tips on healthy foods and told me she was surprised when she was advised not to feed her son take away, until he was old enough to digest it properly. She thought the nappy smell was normal. I beg to differ.

I saw this lady regularly throughout her pregnancy and she did well until she got to 33 weeks. Her waters went whilst she in my clinic and almost immediately her contractions started. I called her partner and an ambulance and whilst waiting for the ambulance, I phoned for another midwife to come and take over at my clinic so that I could accompany her to the hospital in the ambulance. The reception staff were informed of what was going on and told me they would ring the lady's due at clinic to tell them they could have a wait for their appointment.

I informed the delivery suite of what was happening and hoped we would reach the hospital before she delivered, as the baby could at 33 weeks have problems breathing.

Fortunately, the ambulance arrived within ten minutes so I had to abandon my clinic and go to the hospital. I informed the reception staff that another midwife would be with them as soon as possible.

The drive to the hospital was eventful. The lady was contracting every three minutes. She was coping well with the contractions but half way to the unit she had the urge to push. I told the lady to breathe through her contractions and try not to push. This is really difficult for ladies who are getting the urge to push. We got within three miles of the unit when the baby's head was born, quickly followed by the body. Fortunately, with a few rescue breaths the baby started to breathe on its own. We wrapped the baby up in warm towels and gave him to his mother for a cuddle and to help keep him warm. The afterbirth was delivered shortly after this.

When we arrived at the unit we went straight to the delivery suite and the baby was examined by a Paediatrician. The little boy weighed 3 lbs 4 oz and apart from being small was perfect. The lady stayed in hospital for a few days to be with her baby but then went home to be with her other son. She visited her baby on a daily basis and some four weeks later, he was able to go home and join his family.

Thankfully, another midwife had managed to get to Olney and continue with the clinic, although she had taken an hour to get there so four ladies had made appointments for the next clinic.

Then I had to get back to Olney to be reunited with my car. A community midwife who had been working in the unit was good enough to take me.

This lady had another baby after this one and again delivered six weeks early. No reason was found for this to happen so although unusual, it all turned out well in the end.

When I visited this lady at home she proudly told me that she now did all her own cooking and fed her children on proper food. Her words not mine. Bless her, she was a lovely lady and her children were always well behaved and well cared for.

# Interfering Mothers

I was looking after a lovely lady who was having her first baby. She had come for her booking appointment with her mother as her husband was unable to be released from his job to attend.

The mother was very chatty and very excited about the baby being born. It would be a first grandchild for both sets of parents.

The problems started when I was filling in the notes at the booking appointment. As I went through the notes, the mother wanted to comment about every question. She told me that she would be at the birth and that she wished for her daughter to have a caesarean section.

When I asked the lady about this, she told me that her mother had suffered from haemorrhoids (piles) during her pregnancy and after birth and she didn't want this to happen to her daughter. I said it was something that could happen in pregnancy, but if she ate a healthy diet with plenty of fibre this problem could be averted. If she did suffer from this affliction, we could give her some cream to help the situation.

The mother then said that her daughter's diet was good and couldn't be improved. My reply was that's excellent, let's see how the pregnancy progresses.

I eventually finished filling in the notes and then talked to them about the blood tests that we normally did in pregnancy. The lady was happy with this but the mother said her daughter didn't need any blood tests as they knew what blood group she was and as she ate a healthy diet, she was unlikely to be low in iron. With the lady's permission, I was able to take the blood tests with the mother tutting and sighing next to me.

I must admit when the appointment was over I felt exhausted. I arranged to see her at 15 weeks and arranged for her to have a scan at the hospital.

The very next week I had a call from the mother telling me that the scan appointment needed to be changed as she would be unable to attend with her daughter as she was working! I asked her if her daughter was able to attend and was told that was beside the point, it was not convenient to her and as her mother she wanted to be able to be there for the appointment. I had to tell her that it was up to her daughter to ring the scan department, if she was unhappy with the appointment date and time.

When I had finished the conversation, I rang the lady concerned who told me she was happy with the appointment and her husband would be attending with her. I told her that her mother had been on the phone and had asked for the date to be changed. It was news to the girl that her mother had rung me and she apologised and told me that her mother was so into the pregnancy that she wanted to be there for every appointment, but she was happy to go to the scan on the date given. I told her that I would see her after her scan at my clinic.

Well I think her mother had me on speed dial. I had several phone calls from her asking questions about her daughters pregnancy and she went on to tell me that she was unhappy that I had rung her daughter about the scan appointment as she had been unable to accompany her. I apologised but told her I was under the impression that her daughter could not make the appointment. I told her the scan department were extremely busy and although they did their best to meet everybody's needs, they could not always do this.

When the lady was 15 weeks pregnant, I saw that the lady was down for a clinic appointment. I was hoping she would be with her husband and not her mother, so the appointment could go smoothly without any problems.

The lady was the next to be called in when I had a message from the reception staff. The girl's mother was on the phone and said she was running late for the appointment and would I wait until she reached the surgery, before I saw her daughter?

My reaction to this was, actually it was the daughter who had an appointment not her and I felt it would be wrong to leave the lady sitting in the waiting room for nearly an hour until her mother arrived, so I told them that I would be calling the lady in within a few minutes.

I went to fetch the lady from the waiting room and she came in accompanied by her husband. I had to tell her that her mother had phoned and asked me to wait until she got to the surgery.

The lady was shocked and her husband wasn't very happy. I told them that it was their appointment and I was happy to go ahead now. This was accepted.

Everything was fine with the lady and her baby. Her blood results were discussed and then put into her notes and I talked to them about the blood test she could have to see if the baby was at risk of having downs syndrome.

The couple decided they did not want the blood test and I told them that this was fine, it was up to them. They told me that they would go ahead with the pregnancy whatever problem the baby could have. I said this was fine and left it at that. The lady said that her mother wanted her to have the test as she did not want her daughter to have a baby with a problem. I reassured them that this pregnancy was theirs and they should make the decisions they were happy with.

The baby's heartbeat was regular and the couple were delighted to hear it. I suggested that they should record it so that they could let their parents listen to it. This was accepted and once we had checked that it had recorded properly, I talked to them about the next scan that she would be offered at 20 weeks.

Her blood pressure and urine were normal so when I had answered their questions, I arranged to see them after their next scan but told them they could ring me if they had any worries.

Once they had gone, I continued with my clinic then had a phone call from reception telling me that the girl's mother had arrived and was not happy that she had missed the appointment. Just what I wanted to hear. I told them that she should speak to her daughter as it was her appointment and not her mother's.

When I went out to call the next lady, her mother was waiting for me. She was not happy that I had gone ahead with the appointment without her. I told her that I had to keep to appointment times for all the ladies and it would have been difficult to have made them wait for her as that would be over an hour's wait.

The lady told me I should take the grandparents into consideration when I was arranging their appointment, but as I told her the lady had made her own appointment at a time that was convenient to her and had been surprised that her mother had tried to change the time of it.

It was clear the lady was not happy but I told her that we had recorded the baby's heartbeat, so she could listen to it. She grunted and stomped out of the surgery.

My next lady who had heard it all, said I am so glad my mother is not like that, it would drive me mad. I just laughed and said it takes all sorts to make the world go round but it was unusual for a mother to be so involved and want to be at every appointment.

This lady's pregnancy continued normally and when it was time for the ante natal classes to start she told me that she had not told her mother about them and if she rang me would I not divulge to her about them. I must admit this was fine with me so I agreed to do this. She then divulged to me that her mother wanted to be present at the birth but she and her husband did not want her to be there. I told her that this was entirely her choice and nobody would allow her mother in the room if that went again her wishes. The lady was happy with this. I told her it was up to her and her husband to tell who they wanted to that she was in labour and that the labour ward would certainly not be phoning her mother to tell her what was happening.

The classes went off without her mother attending and for that I was truly thankful.

This lady went into labour at 39 weeks and fortunately, it went well and she and her husband had been the only ones present. I saw her the next morning on the ward and she told me that when they had rung her mother to tell her the good news, she had said she was on her way and would stay at her daughters to help look after her for the next few weeks. The lady told me she was dreading her coming as she had fixed ideas about how the baby should be looked after. I told her I would support her as much as I could and it was up to her and her husband how they looked after their baby. She was going home that day, so I arranged to see her the next day.

I arrived at the house and the girl's mother opened the door and invited me in. Her first words were, I think the baby is hungry and needs a bottle. The lady was breastfeeding her baby and apparently, had not fed for long so her mother had suggested a bottle. I told her that I would discuss feeding with her daughter and not to worry.

The lady was coping really well and the baby was pink and looked well. The mother took the baby from her daughter and said that she did not think the baby was being fed properly. I tried to ignore her and talked to the lady about how often and for how long the baby was feeding and was told she was feeding every three hours for approximately twenty mins. I told her that this was great and asked about her nappies. It appeared the baby was doing really well and was passing urine and filling her nappy regularly. The mother interrupted and told me the baby's poo was a funny colour and she thought this meant the baby was hungry.

When babies are first born, their poo is black and sticky, it then goes to a green/black and eventually goes yellow. Breastfed poo is yellow with bits in and runny. Bottle fed baby's poo is like toothpaste. I reassured the mum that the baby was fine and I was not worried at all.

After I had examined the baby, I gave her back to her mother who was delighted with her progress. I told her that I was happy that everything was going well and she would be visited the next day to make sure that all was well. I gave her phone numbers that she could ring if she had any worries.

Then the mother pipes up. I have been to the chemist and brought some formula. I think the baby needs a top up and did I agree? Well actually no, I don't. The baby is a good colour, she is passing urine regularly and is waking up every three hours, the baby is fine. She is contented and acting as a normal healthy baby would.

That went down a storm. I think I know what my granddaughter needs, she told me. I fed her mother with formula and it didn't do her any harm. I told her formula wouldn't harm a baby but it was not necessary with this baby. Babies tummies are very small when they are born and they don't need huge amounts of milk. I felt so sorry for this girl, she was being questioned about everything she did. I reassured her that she was doing beautifully and to carry on as she was doing.

I left telling them I would see them the next day. I was quite pleased to reach my car and have a minute to relax. I found her mother exhausting; it must have been really difficult for her daughter.

When I turned my phone on the next morning, there were three messages from the girl's mother. Each message was a bit more irate. Apparently the baby had woken up after two hours and she was difficult to settle, so the grand mother wanted to give her a bottle. Oh flip, just what I need first thing in the morning.

I made sure that I visited the lady fairly early to make sure that all was well. Again the mother answered the door and was obviously cross that I hadn't answered her phone calls. They were made at 11 pm, 2 and 5 am. I told her I was off duty overnight so my phone had been off.

I went into the lounge to find a tearful mum and a crying baby. I gave her a hug and asked her what her take was on what had happened overnight. She told me the baby had woken up after two hours but when she had tried to settle her, she was difficult to settle. I reassured her and told her that all babies are difficult to settle at some point and it can be for many reasons. They may need some more milk or they could have wind or just need a cuddle. I told the lady I would weigh the baby to make sure that baby was doing well. Usually, babies lose weight in the first few days as they pass a lot of meconium (poo) in the first days of life.

I fetched the scales and fortunately, the baby had not lost but was putting on weight. I congratulated mum on how well she was doing and reassured her that baby was doing very well and didn't need any top ups. The mother of course, disagreed with me and argued that if a bottle was given, the baby would sleep for longer. I told her that this may happen but it wasn't necessary and was against her daughter's wishes. She told me she was upset, I was brainwashing her daughter into breastfeeding. This obviously wasn't the case as her daughter told her. She also told her that she was fed up with her mother interfering and if it continued she would be asking her to go home. Good for her, that is really difficult to stand up to a bossy mother especially when you have just had a baby.

All the checks were fine and I told her that I would be visiting two days later to do the baby's blood test. I hoped that her mother would either have gone home or given her daughter some support.

Thankfully, when I visited two days later, the girl's mother had gone home and her husband was now her support. The lady was doing really well and said she felt so relieved that they were now at home together with their baby. She knew her mum wanted to be involved but had really struggled with all her interference.

I told her she was doing really well and the baby was doing great. She had put on quite a lot of weight and was a good colour and sleeping in between feeds. I reassured her that she was a natural and should carry on as she was doing. I arranged to see her a few days later, but obviously left her with phone number in case she needed any questions answering. Her husband was being very supportive and told me that when he went back to work, his own mother was coming to help. They asked me not to tell her mother if she happened to phone me. I told them their secret was safe with me and not to worry.

I visited some days later and the husband had gone back to work and his mother was there giving support. What a difference, she was great, she didn't interfere and asked them what they wanted her to help with. She left the care of the baby to them and was on hand to help with cooking and cleaning. She had also looked after the baby for a couple of hours so that mum could get some sleep. This is the kind of help that new mums need someone, who will support them but not condemn them for the way they choose to look after their babies.

I was able to discharge this lady and her baby on her tenth day, when she told me that she had had a huge row with her mum over the last few days and thought that when she decided to visit she would be more supportive and put less pressure on her. I do hope that is right. No new mum needs to be questioned about the care they are giving to their baby. I have seen this cause depression in ladies before and it's not helpful at all. I wished the lady well and told her I would see her when she was around and about with her baby.

# Funny Events

I once looked after a lady who was interesting to say the least. She used to come to clinic with her partner and her teddy bear. She was very childlike and seemed to know very little about pregnancy and what was happening to her body. She giggled a lot and seemed to me to be away with the fairies.

I really liked this lady; she was a bit strange but what I call the salt of the earth. She was very excited to be pregnant and seemed to think the baby would be born quite soon. She was ten weeks pregnant, when I first met her and told me that she thought her baby would be born in a couple of months. I explained to her about the length of pregnancy and she seemed very surprised. Her partner always accompanied her but rarely said anything. He seemed very shy and was obviously embarrassed by some of the questions I was asking his partner.

When I was asking about the date of her last period, he started rocking and looked so uncomfortable. I told him that we have to ask certain questions to ascertain when their baby would be due. He grunted at this and said he thought it was rude to talk about periods. Apparently, his parents had told him that this was so. I reassured him that it was normal for all ladies to have periods to which he said, well my mother never did. I answered to this, well if your mother had not had periods you would never have been born. He told me that his mother had told him that sex was off bounds for normal people and you only had periods if you had sex. Phew, how to answer that one. I asked him if he had any sisters or brothers. Yes, he said I have three brothers and a sister. I told him that he should talk to his parents and tell them that they were having a baby. He looked shocked and said that they would think he was sinful if he told them. Oh dear, this is a difficult situation for him. I reassured him that it was very normal to have sex when you love someone and there is nothing dirty about it. All the time I was talking to the partner, the girl was giggling.

It turned out that they had both been brought up in very religious families, who had taught them that sex was a sin.

I eventually managed to carry on with the appointment and found all to be normal. I arranged a scan for her and told her to make an appointment to see me in five weeks when we would be able to listen to the baby's heartbeat. They asked me how I could do this and I showed them the Sonic aid which allows us to do this.

Fortunately, they went off happily. I spoke to their GP about the booking and he told me that they had led a very sheltered life and sometimes found life difficult. He had seen this couple when they had been told about the pregnancy and had been surprised that this had happened but were very happy with the situation. He thought that they would do very well but would need a lot of support.

This lady's pregnancy went well and when it was time for the ante natal classes, I decided that I needed to visit them at home before they started to make sure they would be happy with what was discussed at the classes.

I visited them at home and asked them what they knew about the way their baby would be born. They looked surprised and said the baby would be born out of her belly button. Oh God. I talked to them about the birth process and they were really surprised when I told them that the baby comes out the same way it goes in.

I think I managed to impart enough knowledge that they would need to get them through the birth. I told them about the classes and said they were very welcome to come as they would meet other couples who were having babies and could make some new friends.

They did come to the classes and when I spoke to them after the first class, they told me they had learnt a lot and had enjoyed themselves.

This lady did very well and went into labour when she was 40 weeks pregnant. Apparently, she took her teddy into the hospital with her, she clutched it throughout her labour and coped with the contractions really well. She delivered a beautiful baby boy and I saw them when they arrived home.

They were coping well with the baby and asked me what I thought of their choice of name. They wanted to call their baby Dumbo. Ugh, not sure about that I said, have you got any other names in mind. They told me they wanted to call their baby after a Disney character to which I replied that's fine but you have to keep in mind that the baby would have the name for life and they didn't want him to be teased when he went to school. I told them to have a think about it as they had six weeks to register the birth.

I was talking to the GP about the couples name for the baby and he laughed. I told him I had told them to think of another name but it was obviously up to them what they named their baby. I suppose it's better than Pinocchio, but I didn't think the registrar would allow Dumbo. The GP told me I had made his day and he would wait with bated breath to be told the final name.

When I visited the couple they had talked about the baby's name and had decided to call him Trevor.

Well that was a relief, but I can't remember a Disney character called Trevor.

This couple did really well, the baby thrived and apparently their parents had been pleased about his birth and had visited them. The couple had talked to them about the lack of knowledge they had been given by them and were told that they had done what they thought was right at the time. That's all a parent can do. Hopefully this little boy will be given enough knowledge to allow him to make his own decisions on such important things.

I was able to discharge this lady at the normal time and hand over her care to the health visitor.

# Wrong Sex

I had a lovely couple who were expecting their first baby. They were so excited and very keen to learn about pregnancy and birth. I talked through the notes with them asking where they would like to deliver their baby. They had talked this through and decided they wanted a home birth. I told them that I was happy with this as long as they had no problems during their pregnancy.

Bloods were taken and a scan appointment was made for them. I also talked to them about the anomaly scan. This is usually done at around 20 weeks and it makes sure that the baby is well and has no problems. Parents can also find out the sex of their baby which this couple were keen to do.

I arranged to see them at 15 weeks telling them they could ring me if they had any worries or problems.

This couple had a very normal pregnancy. They were delighted to be having a daughter. They told me that only girls were ever born in their family so they were not surprised. They asked me if this was a hundred per cent that their baby was a girl. I told them that we couldn't give them a written guarantee but it was rare for the scan department to be wrong. They were happy with this and I arranged to see them at their next appointment.

I was lucky enough to be around when this couple went into labour. I arrived at the house to find a very excited husband. The lady had been having contractions regularly and was doing very well. Her blood pressure, temperature and pulse were fine. On examination she was 5 cm dilated, so half way there. I encouraged her to move around and rest between contractions.

Her labour went very well and several hours later, she was feeling pressure so I offered to examine her. She was agreeable to this and we found that she was 8 cm dilated so was doing really well.

I told them I would ring for the second midwife and that she should carry on as she was doing. I encouraged her to have something to eat so that she would have the energy to push when time came. This was agreed and she had a chocolate bar and a sugary drink.

The second midwife arrived some time later and was surprised that this first-time mum was doing so well.

Some two hours later, she felt the urge to push. We told her to do what her body was telling her to do. All the equipment was ready for the delivery so we just sat back and waited for the baby to put in an appearance.

Within twenty minutes, the baby's head was born quickly followed by the body. I passed the baby to the mum and when the cord had been cut by dad he suddenly said. Oh my god, our daughter has a penis. I had already noticed that it was a boy but had left it to the parents to see this for themselves. I reassured him that his daughter had not got a penis but in fact they had given birth to a son.

The poor husband was so shocked but really happy. They commented that they were glad they had not bought everything pink. They were really happy with their baby but had to have a rethink on the name as they had wanted to call the baby Lucy. I said they could always change it to Louis, but they had plenty of time to think of the name.

Whilst we were clearing up and drinking a nice cup of tea, the dad decided to ring both parents. They were wondering how they would react to the news that they had a grandson. I told them they would be happy whatever and pleased that the birth had gone well.

The notes were filled in and once the lady was back in her bed with her son feeding, we left them with telephone numbers telling them that a midwife would visit them that afternoon.

I visited this couple the next day and they were thrilled with their baby. Apparently their parents had been very shocked but delighted with their grandson. They both told them that they would have to return the clothes they had bought back to the shop to change them for a different colour.

This couple did very well and they were thrilled with their son. They said when they had another baby they would not find out the sex as they had been so pleased with their surprise son that they would like a surprise the next time.

It was lovely to see this couple so happy with their baby and not even a bit cross that about the wrong sex call.

It is very rare that the scan department get it wrong, but nothing is impossible. I can only think of one other couple that had this happen to them and that was at a different hospital. They were told they were having a girl and surprise it was a boy. This couple decorated the nursery pink and everything else was pink. When they delivered a boy, they tried to sue the scan department at their hospital. I did tell them that their baby would not care what colour the nursery was as long as it was warm and comfortable. Nothing came of this as parents should be aware that we can't guarantee anything.

The mum and baby did very well, the baby gained a lot of weight and the breastfeeding went very well. I was able to discharge them into the care of the health visitor when the baby was ten days old.

# Caravan Delivery

I was called out one night to a home birth in a village at the other side of Milton Keynes. I was given the address and was told that the lady lived on a caravan site and that the husband would meet me at the entrance.

Well this was a first, I had never delivered a baby in a caravan before, but made my way to the area and was met by the husband. He pointed out the caravan I needed to get to and was invited in.

The caravan was tiny. There was a really small kitchen, a narrow passageway that let into a lounge and then a bedroom, where a lady was laying obviously in labour. There was very little room around the bed and it was difficult to get around the room.

There wasn't anywhere to put our equipment and I thought to myself, *this is going to be fun*. I talked to the lady and asked her about her contractions, how frequent and how long and painful they were? I was told the contractions were coming every three minutes and were lasting about 45 seconds and were very painful.

I was able to take her blood pressure, temperature and pulse and then I asked her if I could examine her. She was reluctant for this to happen and I must admit, I groaned to myself and thought *here we go again.* It is difficult to know what is happening during labour if we don't know how dilated the lady is.

I explained this to her and she told me that she didn't let anyone examine her internally and she wasn't changing her mind on this occasion. Oh God, *why do they do this to us midwives?* This was the ladies first baby so she didn't really know what to expect.

I asked her if she had been seen when she was 36 weeks to discuss the birth and she told me that the midwife had done this at the surgery. Well, that wasn't very helpful as we need to see that the premises are safe and suitable for a home birth.

I then asked if she had told her midwife that she didn't want any vaginal examinations and was told no she didn't ask her. I inquired if she had been to any ante natal classes and was told no as she didn't think she needed them.

At ante natal classes, women learn about what happens in labour? how they can help themselves and what the methods of pain relief are.

It was agreed that we would watch and wait and as long as the baby's heart beat remained stable and everything else was going well we would carry on and see how she went.

The lady was lying flat on her back and I advised her to either sit up or get onto all fours so that her baby's head was pressing on her cervix to help it to dilate. Well the answer to this was I am comfortable as I am. Well that's okay then.

I was offered a cup of tea which I gratefully took and asked the lady where she wanted to deliver?

This lady wanted to deliver on the bed, which is fine but I could see already that the lady was becoming distressed with her contractions. She was asking to use the gas and air. I explained to her that this was available but we only carried two small tanks which on average lasted about half an hour each. The problem was I did not know how dilated she was so it was difficult to ascertain when she should use it.

Sometime later, her waters went and they were stained brown. This shows that the baby has had a bowel movement, which can mean the baby could inhale this at the delivery. I explained this to the couple but they were reluctant to be transferred into the hospital.

The husband told me that her mother lived in one of the adjacent caravans and that he would go and fetch her so that they had some more support. I told him this was fine but unless she was a midwife or obstetrician, this was not necessary.

The answer to this was, I am fetching her. I did wonder where she was going to stand as the room was already at bursting point.

The mother arrived and informed me that whatever I said, they were going to stay at home as this is what they wanted. Well that's alright then. I explained to the mother about what was going on and told her because I had not examined her, I did not know how the labour was progressing.

Needless to say, there were three happy people in the room and one midwife who was quite frustrated about what was going on. I told them that I was ringing the hospital to let them know how things were going and to tell them that the baby had had a bowel movement. They were not happy about this but I told them that I had to let them know as if they would not transfer to the hospital then I would need to get a second midwife to assist at the birth.

I phoned the hospital and told them I didn't need a second midwife yet but would let them know when I did. By this time, dawn was breaking and it was becoming light outside.

The baby's heartbeat remained stable for which I was truly grateful. She actually was very calm and composed and appeared to be progressing well.

It was at this point that I noticed there were no curtains at the windows. I asked them if they had anything to cover them. They seemed surprised by my request and said no they didn't feel the need for curtains.

Sometime later, the lady said she wanted to push. I phoned the hospital and asked them to send the second midwife.

It was at this point that the lady started screaming. She was so loud it hurt my ears, but I offered her the gas and air and she was thankful to start using it. This calmed her down somewhat and I asked her again if I could examine her. No you can't she said, in chorus with her husband and mother. I tried to explain to them that I did not want her to push on a cervix that was not fully dilated but this fell on deaf ears.

Thankfully, shortly after this the second midwife arrived and I met her at the door and filled her in on what was going on. There was a lot of eye rolling from the midwife and I just said we need to make sure this baby does not inhale meconium. Fortunately, the lady was fully dilated and shortly after this the baby's head was visible. We arranged our equipment as best as we could in the tight space and waited for the baby to put in an appearance.

All of a sudden, the second midwife whispered to me that we have an audience. I turned round and there were several people staring in the windows of the caravan. I told the family about the people watching and they ignored me, so I thought to myself let's just get this baby delivered.

The lady started pushing and the head was delivered. I held the baby's chin up so that it couldn't breathe in any of the meconium. The cord was loosely around the neck so this was unravelled and with a final push, the baby was born to cheers from outside. They were all shouting what sex is it? The husband shouted it's a boy. Well actually, it's a girl I said. The husband did a double take and said well what's this then? The cord I told him. He just turned round and shouted it's a girl. All I could hear was noise from outside. Some of which was funny. Ugh, that was gross, if that's childbirth I am never having a baby.

The placenta was delivered safely and thankfully the baby was fine. I told them that usually after a birth including meconium, the baby was observed in hospital for at least twenty-four hours. They were not happy for this to happen so I told them that they needed to keep a close eye on their baby and we would ask a midwife to visit them that afternoon to make sure all was well.

Fortunately, the lady did not need any stitches and her blood loss was minimal. The mother said I knew they would be fine and didn't need to go into hospital, you midwives always frighten people about what could happen and it doesn't.

I thought this was not worth answering but the other midwife told them they were very lucky that they had no problems and it could have been a different story.

We wrote our notes and helped the mum breastfeeding. We then asked her if she wanted a shower or a bath and were informed they didn't have washing facilities on the caravan.

They had a small toilet but no shower or basin. The only sink was in the kitchen. I asked the husband if they had a bowl we could fill with water to help her to have a wash. The answer was no, she is fine she doesn't need a wash.

Poor woman, after having a baby it's really nice to have a shower or bath and then get into bed. Apparently they went into her mother's caravan for a shower when they needed one.

We asked if they had any clean sheets so that we could make the bed clean for her and were informed they hadn't. Oh flip, I asked the mother if she had any clean linen that we could use. I was told she had no spare linen, but would strip her daughter's bed and take it to the launderette. Well that would have to do.

Once the lady was settled and the baby had fed, we left her with telephone numbers and told her to ring those numbers if she had any problems.

That afternoon, a midwife visited and was not happy with the baby. Apparently she was grunting and her nose was flaring. She phoned the paediatrician at the hospital who advised that the baby she be sent into hospital in case she had an infection. Unfortunately, the lady and her husband were not happy about this and did not want to go in. They were told that the baby could become very ill if they did not take their baby into the hospital.

Fortunately, the lady agreed to be admitted with her baby and the mother took her in. One of the girl's mother's comments on hearing that the baby was to be admitted was, I knew that old bat (me) wanted the baby in hospital. I hope she will be happy now.

The midwife told her it was nothing to do with me but it was just unfortunate that the baby appeared unwell, which probably meant she had inhaled some of the meconium.

This baby was admitted to the special care baby unit and was administered intravenous antibiotics. She was quite poorly for a few days but fortunately, she was able to go home after a week. I even got a thank you card from the couple thanking me for delivering their baby. Thank goodness, it turned out well in the end.

I have been so lucky in my career to have delivered so many babies. No two births are the same and it makes for a very interesting life.

All community midwives need a good back up plan and I have for the most part been very lucky in the support I have got from my lovely colleagues.

The areas I have worked in have been varied and interesting and I have met some really lovely people. The mothers and babies I have been lucky enough to meet and work with have been lovely. I feel very blessed to have had such a long happy career. Without the support of my lovely husband and family, this would not have been possible.